FROM ALCOHOLISM TO SERENITY

Jacques Turgeon

MÉDIASPAUL

First published as *De l'alcoolisme à la paix et à la sérénité,* Leméac
éditeur, Montréal, 1987. Translated from the French by Angele Morino,
F.J., and Bianca Zagolin.

Canadian Cataloguing in Publication Data

Turgeon, Jacques, 1929-1993

   From Alcoholism to Serenity

   Translation of: De l'alcoolisme à la paix et à la sérénité.

   ISBN 2-89420-321-7

   1. Conduct of life. 2. Christian life. 3 Suffering —
Religious aspects. 4. Alcoholism — Religious aspects. I. Title.

BJ1482.J3213 1996   248.4   C96-940031-4

Phototypesetting : *Médiaspaul*

Cover : *Boulerice & Morissette*

ISBN 2-89420-321-7

Legal Deposit — 2nd Quarter 1996
Bibliothèque nationale du Québec
National Library of Canada

© 1996 Médiaspaul
          250, boul. St-François Nord
          Sherbrooke, QC, J1E 2B9 (Canada)

To those I love; many are they!

For their support and their advice, my sincere thanks to Paule C., Gilles C., Francine G., René G., Léon M., Lionel G., Lucie L., Léandre et Lucille.

The Author

CONTENTS

FOREWORD

In spite of its title, this book is not the account of a life ruined by alcohol. Alcoholism is but the starting point of self-awareness, of a change of attitude toward life, its values, its meaning. More than anything else, it is about the art of discovering within oneself the seed of the Kingdom.

This work is dedicated to all those who suffer and feel isolated, those who search in vain for an answer to life. To all the wretched of the earth, the Kingdom has been promised. Alcohol is only one of the escapes life offers from difficulties and stress: drugs, medication, gambling, self-centredness, resentment are all negative reactions to the bitter struggle that is life. But these, only provide temporary relief, and sooner or later we must face the fact: the escape will become more unbearable than reality. We will then have reached the **limit**.

But there are many other limits in life : homeliness, physical and psychological infirmities, terminal diseases like cancer, the decease of a loved one, in short, anything which causes extreme suffering and over which we have no control. It then seems—and wrongly so—that the only remedy to these sufferings would be to transform ugliness into beauty, illness into physical fitness, death into resurrection. In other words, the panacea for all our sorrows would be the miracle solution which would restore sight to the blind and raise the dead to life.

I am in no way denying the possibility of miracles, but there are without a doubt very few resurrected people walking our streets since the time of Lazarus!

But there is another solution. It is the transformation of the inner self at the level of "being". It is the very way in which we live our deficiencies that must change. I myself must change. And that implies a change from the inside out. That is exactly what this book is all about.

The method I am suggesting emanates from the programme for Alcoholics Anonymous of which I have been a member for twenty years; that explains my wish to remain anonymous, not because I am ashamed to be an alcoholic, but rather to comply with the tradition of A.A. which suggests working behind the scenes without seeking personal fame.

In its recovery programme, A.A. suggests turning to God, but to "God as we understood Him". One's beliefs about God are strictly personal and are not the concern of the Association. This freedom of "a God, as we understood Him" is very precious. When I seriously determined to join A.A., I had already, a few days earlier, in a psychiatric ward, experienced a profound religious encounter with the God of my childhood. I was very appreciative that no one tried to discuss my personal way of seeing the Absolute.

Alcoholics Anonymous further suggests that each one should try to recognize his or her deficiencies, the harm one has done to others, and to share this with someone, until it becomes possible to make amends for that harm. This is very much like the self-examination we practised in college under the guidance of a spiritual director. I was a boarder then, doing classical studies; our educators would emphasize the importance of prayer and meditation, exercises also recommended by A.A. Which means—as I write in this book—that the originality of the A.A. programme is more one of form than one of substance.

Moreover, A.A. has never claimed that, before it was founded in 1935, no individual had ever been able to find God through his suffering, nor that no one had ever reflected on his shortcomings and shared them with someone. As for prayer and meditation, history would surely be powerless to reveal which tribe or people first used them.

What are some of the advantages of the A.A. programme if its basic form is as old as the world itself? The programme is divided into stages or steps of development numbered 1 to 12, and offers all the advantages of a "spiritual methodology", so to speak. As a result, to have reached one of the stages is a milestone in the spiritual progression, and it makes the followers of the programme extremely conscious of the step forward they have taken. When nine steps have been completed, the remaining three provide additional drill for the first nine, thus ensuring the continued application of the method.

If I propose the A.A. plan, it is because I myself have evolved spiritually "starting from" the suggestions contained in the principles of A.A. I say "starting from" these suggestions, because my spiritual evolution and its general direction were marked by my personal way of seeing God. The latter was instrumental in my growth far beyond the point where A.A.—as an association— was able to follow me. In fact, A.A. must not—that remains one of its strongest assets—go beyond "God, as we understood Him."

What I will share here is my experience as a Christian during my years at A.A. This association has no part in the publication of this book, and is in no way implicated. However, Alcoholics Anonymous has never been opposed to anything which can be of service to alcoholics, as in the case of the outstanding work of Joseph Kessel.

I invite my reader, whoever he may be, to discover in these pages a reason for his suffering, his solitude, his isolation. For in the final analysis, has an alcoholic ever suffered from anything else? Besides, the Alcoholics Anonymous book, often called the *Big Book*, reminds its readers: "I know of no human activity to which the 12 steps cannot be applied usefully." Friends of mine, sincere Christian who had never experienced tragedy in their lives, decided, for reasons of personal development, to go through each of the steps of the A.A. programme, including the moral inventory and the help to others through visits to the poor and the ill. This confirms what A.A. foresaw twenty-five years ago and which is also expressed in the *Big Book*: "I believe that the A.A. movement can influence the world even more than it has so far and that it will greatly contribute to the spiritual reawakening that has begun..." And that is precisely my reason for writing this book.

Besides, the doctor, social worker, nurse, personnel director, all those who want to help alcoholics, will certainly benefit from reading these pages. In particular, members of Al-Anon, for whom I have such great esteem and affection, will want to acquaint themselves with this book.

For those who may not know what Al-Anon means, the word comes from AL-coholics and ANON-ymous, and might suggest: non A.A., or NON AL-coholics, as I have been told. This Family Movement brings together the spouses, the adult children, the fathers and mothers, other family members and friends, in short, all those who live close to an alcoholic or to a person with an alcohol problem. Al Anon offers the same programme of spiritual renewal as A.A., emphasizing the same principles summarized in the 12 steps which I shall discuss later.

The Alateen Movement—similar to Al-Anon—is for children too young to join adult groups. They too will want to read this book.

Finally—it goes without saying—to the members of A.A., Gamblers Anonymous, Overeaters Anonymous... To those still struggling with alcohol... To those who search... To all the "poor"—this book I offer.

"Blessed are the poor... those who suffer... those who weep..." You have doubtless recognized the Beatitudes. Contradictory? Not at all. Paradoxical? Most certainly.

Jacques Turgeon

THE LIMIT

That there are in our lives events completely beyond our control is very evident: death, amputation of a limb, the loss of precious heirlooms in a fire... Yet as irrefutable as is our powerlessness in the face of such hardships—our limits—they are hotly debated as though we could do something about them. Denial is not so much the inability to face reality as the lack of inner strength to "accept it". The difficulty then is not in "seeing" or "admitting" our limits in themselves, but in "accepting" them.

Other limits, just as obvious, are not an immediate concern because we can push them back: for example, we can hide aging by the use of cosmetics, or delay it by surgery. Other limits can sometimes be completely overcome, but that is because they were never real limits to begin with: a poor man may become rich; a very sick person may recover perfect health. To overcome a limiting situation presupposes that we refuse to "accept" it, that we will use all the means at our disposal to rise above it: courage, self-sacrifice, tenacity, even heroism if need be. Such an attitude reveals the dignity and grandeur of a human being. But how many such struggles, as admirable as they may be, have, alas, proved to be useless and extenuating; we fail to rise above our limits. The problem is therefore one of distinguishing between those situations which can be changed and those which cannot. Alcoholics Anonymous, having understood the vital importance of such a distinction, has made its own this beautiful prayer:

"My God, give me the serenity to accept the things I cannot change, the courage to change those I can, and the wisdom to know the difference."

This prayer is said before each meeting. As I have said, this book is dedicated to all those who suffer, who feel isolated, those who are searching for answers but to no avail. Among these, the alcoholics are some of the most afflicted; the struggle against alcoholism is hard, anguishing and exhausting. It is of this limit I wish to speak. Being an alcoholic, I almost lost myself completely in the abyss. I was able to recover thanks to the principles of inner life. These principles are clearly outlined by A.A. in its "Twelve Steps". They are simple in themselves, but the road they would have us follow is very difficult! It is a road we must travel from deep inside ourselves, and it leads to the door of true happiness. If these principles can bring consolation and peace to alcoholics, they can surely alleviate all other sorrows.

However, a few remarks would be in order here. When reading about the twelve steps, you cannot fail to notice the use of the word "God", as well as references to prayer and meditation. It may be that this will leave you indifferent, or please you; if this is the case, then there is no problem. But if each time you hear about God, prayer and meditation, you react negatively and think to yourself: "More pious nonsense!", I understand you perfectly! Especially if you are on the wrong side of forty. You probably remember an outdated religious upbringing, full of: "Thou shalt nots", precepts, rituals, all of which brought more anxiety than peace, more rejection than compassion. Luckily, this education is outmoded today, and so much the better for those who now receive more open-minded teachings. But this new outlook does nothing for us—you and me—who have heard more decrees than callings to rise beyond ourselves in the name of a God whose kindness and friendship brought him to his knees to wash our feet! Let me reassure you: no one is trying to take you back to the structures you have known, or to integrate you into a prayer group, or to impose anything on you. It is enough for now to believe that nature does not emanate from us, that the cosmos is not our doing, and that we are not at the origin of Creation. If you agree, then it follows that there could perhaps exist something or someone greater than we are. In the A.A. steps, this someone "greater than we are" is called "Supreme Being" or "God, as each one conceives of Him". As for prayer and meditation, it simply means to start a dialogue by uttering a phrase as simple as: "Help me." This could be for you the beginning of a new life!

The following is the text of the twelve steps:

1. We admitted we were powerless over alcohol—that our lives had become unmanageable.

2. Came to believe that a Power greater than ourselves could restore us to sanity.

3. Made a decision to turn our will and our lives over to the care of a God, *as we understood Him.*

4. Made a searching and fearless moral inventory of ourselves.

5. Admitted to God, to ourselves and to another human being the exact nature of our wrongs.

6. Were entirely ready to have God remove all these defects of character.

7. Humbly asked Him to remove our shortcomings.

8. Made a list of all persons we have harmed, and became willing to make amends to them all.

9. Made direct amends to such people wherever possible, except when to do so would injure them or others.

10. Continued to take personal inventory and when we were wrong promptly admitted it.

11. Sought through prayer and meditation to improve our conscious contact with God *as we understood Him*, praying only for knowledge of His will for us and the power to carry that out.

12. Having had a spiritual awakening as a result of these steps, we tried to carry this message to alcoholics, and to practise these principles in all our affairs.

As you read these steps, what impression did they make on you? Let me share with you my reaction when —nearly thirty years ago—I read this text for the first time. I was keenly disappointed; I felt as though I had been transported back to the religion of my childhood, and literally dropped "in church". I was shocked. "They are all a little touched in the head" I thought! Why did I react that way? I shall try to answer in the next few pages.

I would ask you not to go back to reread the text of the twelve steps, especially if you have no experience of A.A. In fact, this numbered series may seem little more to you than a list of precepts which require blind obedience. But, of course, there is much more to it than that, since it outlines the steps of a spiritual journey. It is my own personal experience that I am offering here; and since you have bought the book, I ask you humbly that you trust me.

We shall travel along together on that journey, that is, cover the ground of twenty-eight years of experience, during which I endeavoured to cover these steps. Twenty-eight years of searching and shared reflection. The steps must be adjusted to each individual life, that is, given a specific content that A.A. did not provide on purpose. It is not an easy task, yet it is indispensable. Once again, the direction I will give them will be one of my own choosing and will not commit the association of Alcoholics Anonymous to anything. In fact, any member of A.A. can give them the direction he wishes. This freedom is granted in the phrase: "God, as we understood Him."

You will have noticed that, in these first pages, I have referred to the "alcoholic", or any person having an "alcohol problem". This distinction is important. Some people willingly admit having "a problem" with alcohol, that their drinking habits are disastrous, and that they must do something about them. Yet they would never admit for one moment that they might be "alcoholics". The word offends them. Indeed, for many people, the word "alcoholic" has a very unpleasant psychological connotation. This stems from our education. Alcoholism was for too long reguarded as a terrible, shameful vice that we must "cover up" rather than the illness that it is.

And I am not totally convinced that all right-thinking people, doctors, psychiatrists, educators, acknowledge alcoholism to be an illness. But, even if that were the case, some still consider many diseases as "shameful". So we would be no further ahead.

On the other hand, a person may admit to being an alcoholic, but think that he will recover on his own. If that person is really an alcoholic, then he is doomed to fail miserably. Hence, the important question is not whether that person is an "alcoholic", or whether he has a problem with "alcohol", but whether he can solve the problem on his own, by himself, either by regulating the amount of alcohol consumed, or by abstaining completely. He will have to try both of these solutions. If he is unable to achieve a permanent cure, he is an alcoholic. In my humble opinion, an alcoholic is not someone who drinks disastrous amounts of alcohol, but someone who cannot, when he so wishes, stop drinking altogether. Why all the fuss? If you are not an alcoholic, and alcohol is disturbing you, then quit drinking! Nothing simpler than that, right? I tried it for ten years. My record for abstaining? Two months! I boasted to all who would listen that I could stop drinking whenever I willed it! The only snag was that I could never will it for a very long time.

Part one

ACCEPTING
WHAT WE CANNOT CHANGE

Much of our suffering often comes from our inability to accept situations which we are powerless to change. I shall explain this by referring to step one of Alcoholics Anonymous. Why A.A.? Because A.A. has been so successful in its treatment of alcoholics that it holds meetings in over one hundred countries. An exact number of those who abstain from alcohol because of A.A. is not available, but it is close to one million. These statistics cannot be matched by any other organization of its kind, and I am here reminded of a quotation from the Bible: "By their fruit you shall know them." Here then is Step one:

"We admitted we were powerless over alcohol—that our lives had become unmanageable." In other words, the day came when we had to face that one fact: the impossibility of ever finding a solution to our alcohol problem. Moreover, our drinking led to other problems which we could no longer—or soon no longer—cope with. In life we face many such situations, sorrows we must learn to accept because we cannot do anything about them. Those who do not have an alcohol problem have but to replace the word "alcohol" with any other cause of intense suffering, and admit their powerlessness to change their condition.

We should do well to remember that the first step does not consist primarily in admitting that one is an alcoholic, but rather in ackowledging that one is "powerless", that is "unable", utterly incapable of overcoming an alcohol problem. Of course, someone who admits being an alcoholic, or having a serious problem with alcohol, is far ahead of someone who doesn't even realize that his drinking is out of control. But clearly it is not enough. It stands repeating that, while someone may acknowledge his condition, he may still believe himself capable of handling his own problem. "Why not?" you will ask. "There are countless specialists: psychologists, psychiatrists, therapists specializing in alcoholism. What about psychoanalysis? Hypnotism has been known to work." Many of us have tried some, or all, of these approaches, and have certainly benefited from them; yet for some unknown reason, we failed to throw off the yoke. These various therapies are not held to be "harmful" but rather "inadequate."

I do not mean to imply that, having resolved his alcohol problem, an A.A. member should refrain, in other areas, from consulting specialists for treatment. We all think that A.A. members should consult their doctors were they to suffer from a bilious attack, and by the same token, they should consult a specialist when they feel a violent and persistent desire to commit suicide. For A.A. members not only succeed in overcoming their craving for alcohol, but also in forming enriching friendships, in helping other alcoholics and, generally speaking, in returning—at least on the outside—to a life much like everybody else's. Should a member suffer from schizophrenia or paranoia, or from some other serious psychic disorder he would, while pursuing his A.A. activities, still consult a specialist for the above-mentioned problems. It would be a serious mistake—if not a fatal one—to claim that the A.A. steps will cure any mental illness.

Back to our subject! In order to give you a vivid illustration of what A.A. means when speaking of "powerlessness" reguarding alcohol, let me tell you briefly how I came to admit "my absolute powerlessness" to reduce my alcohol consumption or stop drinking for good. I must have been twenty-two or twenty-three years old when I first admitted to being an alcoholic. It wasn't very difficult. In the first place, I was always drunk! Besides, I felt no shame in acknowledging the fact. I had the privilege to grow up in a milieu that did not dramatize everything. I was not taught by my family to "oh" and "ah" about anything out of the ordinary, so that I never learned that it was shameful to be an alcoholic. I was taken by ambulance to a small clinic for alcoholics. My years of drinking had weakened my constitution because I ate as little as possible; beer replaced lunch and I skipped dinner very often. Moreover I worked hard in a commercial enterprise of which I was the owner. Eating seemed a trivial, primitive, animal-like activity. I ate only when my hunger was so strong that I could no longer go without food. Eating always lowered the "high" provided by liquor, and I would always put it off. This explains the ambulance trip at a relatively early age. In this clinic, I met a very compassionate doctor. He welcomed me with more concern and kindness that I could ever have hoped for, and I never think of Dr. Alexandre Bédard without a deep sense of gratitude.

I still remember the first conversation which I had with him.

— You are very young to have come to this clinic, and in such a state. Do you know that you were brought here in an ambulance?

— No, Sir, but where am I?

— You are in a clinic for alcoholics and I am your doctor, Dr. Bédard.

I was speechless from shock, and the good doctor continued:

— You doubtlessly know that you were dead drunk... and not being used to it...

— But, Doctor, I intervened, I always drink like that... and I think I have become an alcoholic.

I had no trouble admitting that I was an alcoholic. But believe me, that didn't stop me from drinking. In the light of several other conversations with me, Dr. Bédard was led to confirm that I was an alcoholic. He had treated many for years and had no doubts about me. I was in total agreement with him, having known myself for a while. When I asked Dr. Bédard his remedy for curing alcoholism, he said: "I have none." Then he discussed with me the importance of never taking alcohol in any form whatsoever; that one glass of beer could be seriously harmful. He was very demanding: total abstinence, nothing less. Two weeks later, I was discharged from the clinic.

Anybody knows—one doesn't have to be a genius to understand this—that if an alcoholic were once and for all to refrain from drinking, his alcohol problem would disappear. This is hardly earth-shattering news! And so I thought that everything would be fine: all I had to do was stop drinking! How could I not see that before? It was so simple: just stop drinking! How wonderful life was going to be! What a liberation! No more binges... no more wasted money... no more hangovers... no more foolish behaviour! I would retire early, take my business seriously, go to concerts, travel, read, listen to music. I would be well dressed—I had the means to be—and I would buy a nice car! If you only knew how I enjoyed making all these plans! How sound and reasonable they seemed! At long last, I was going to be happy!

But I soon discovered that "deciding" to live without alcohol was one thing, abstaining quite another! What misery! The very next day after leaving the clinic, I started a campaign of persuasion on myself: "Remember what the doctor said, Jacques, you can't drink... you are an alcoholic, as you well know. Make yourself a good cup of coffee. Not everyone takes alcohol for breakfast. You are no worse off that those who take only coffee." I would then go to the kitchen and make myself a cup of coffee: "You see, Jacques, it doesn't taste that bad." Then, I would go to the washroom and glance in the mirror: "See, your eyes are still red... you are very thin... if you quit drinking, you will put on weight, your eyes will brighten up... it's so much better not to drink... get yourself another cup of coffee." I had become obsessed with the idea and could think of nothing else. I kept looking at my watch and babbling: "It's ten o'clock... you got up at eight and you haven't had a drink in two hours. Aren't you pleased with yourself?" And I drank juices... pop... and more coffee until lunch time. "Excellent" I thought. "The morning is over. It wasn't that bad, was it? Hang in there, don't give in. How about going to the restaurant and ordering a good meal?" I would be off to the restaurant, repeating to myself that it was better not to take wine... that I was an alcoholic... I knew it... that the Doctor had confirmed my condition... that I would be much happier... that drinking and not eating was not much of a life... that I had to resist... I had promised myself... that my happiness depended on it. I ordered a meal with neither wine nor liquor. As I left the restaurant, I congratulated myself: "Aren't you proud of yourself? Just you wait and see, this day is going to fly faster than you think." But the afternoon was still before me. Same little game: looking at my watch, congratulating myself, drinking juice, coke, coffee... firmly convinced I was an alcoholic and the only rational thing to do was to avoid alcohol. The point is: I *knew* it was best for me not to drink. Any fool could understand that! I still had to face dinner: I kept on rambling. Then evening! What a day! I couldn't very well meet my pals at the pub; that would have been throwing myself into the lion's jaws. So I listened to records, played the piano, watched T.V., drank coffee, coke, juice, all the while telling myself that this was happiness, real life, stability, in other words, heaven! I would go to bed around midnight, completely exhausted! Believe me, nothing can ever be as exhausting as a day spent like that.

The next day, I followed the same routine: coffee, babbling to myself, morning, lunch, afternoon, dinner, evening. After two or three weeks of this, I thought to myself: "I have had enough. I shall perhaps try again next year; but right now I have had it." And off I went to the pub. What a relief! How stupid I had been to believe that life could be worth living without a stop at the tavern, or without meeting my friends at a bar, to hear people bellow, surrounded by noise, music, singing. From now on, things would be much more pleasant. I knew I was an alcoholic: all I had to do was be careful. It would be so nice indeed to just have a few drinks—

not many—just enough to get in a party mood. Surely that was the solution: the happy medium. That's it! The happy medium! How could I have drunk for so long without watching the amount I was drinking? That had been my mistake; anyone would easily have drowned in the amounts of liquor I had consumed. I would have to watch myself. Besides, had I not often heard people say: "Thanks, that's enough; I don't want to overdo it." I would do likewise: learn to say no when I had had enough. And, would you believe it? It worked... exactly four days! Then rallying from a hangover, I told myself that I hadn't watched my drinking closely enough. I decided to be extra careful. A few months later, I was back at Doctor Bédard's Clinic.

I was desperate, but comforted by the thought that I could talk once more with the Doctor. I told him about my being alone, of my wish to live and be happy, with all the clumsiness of those who do not know what they are talking about when they speak of happiness. Sensing the depth of my distress, he sat on the edge of my bed so as not to have to raise his voice to be heard: "I should like to ask you a question. Have you ever thought of turning to prayer... How shall I say... to a spiritual experience? You are so young, you can't have forgotten..." I don't remember if I answered. But I recall distinctly thinking: "Poor fellow! It is very nice of him to wish to comfort me... He's not that old... how can he still think that way?" And I felt that the doctor, for lack of something better, had uttered to console me words that are meant for hopeless cases. Needless to say, I did not follow his advice. My search, as we shall see, continued for ten years. But I wish to add that Doctor Bédard is the only man of science of all those I consulted who was able to give me the right answer. I wish to pay homage to him.

How could I know that the Doctor was right? I was so hopeful of finding another solution. I had not yet tapped all the resources available to me: were not psychology and psychiatry supposed to work wonders? Furthermore, I was only an alcoholic; I wasn't raving mad. A good specialist would cure me in no time at all.

In the meantime, I completely abstained from alcohol. But more and more I felt alone and unhappy, until I decided to put off for another year—perhaps—all my nice plans. I went back to drinking, determined to be doubly careful. I watched myself constantly. To no avail. More and more intoxicated, I ate less and less and roamed from one bar to another, lonely and isolated, in a state of utter confusion. At my wits'end, I decided to drop everything and devote my energies to only one task: through consultation, come to grips, once and for all, with my alcohol problem.

Again, the first thing to do before undertaking my new project was to stop drinking. Abstention was becoming very painful for me. I could never sleep for more than half an hour at a time over a period of seven or eight days. I would wake up with a start sweating profusely, and I recall throwing off a sheet which plopped to the ground like a wet rag. At other times, I would find myself on all fours on my bed, trying to find something to grasp, so fast was my room spinning around me, and I with it. It was like being at the center of a merry-go-round gone out of control. All this would last a long time, and I remember crying like a child while waiting for the whirling to stop. For those eight days, it was useless trying to light a cigarette: one puff and I would start throwing up. I would shake for three or four days on end. I held on to one reassuring thought: I wasn't in any danger, and from day to day things would get better. This wasn't the first time I had stopped drinking and I was beginning to have experience on the subject. When I had fully recovered, I consulted the Telephone Directory under "alcoholism" and spotted "Alcoholics Anonymous" at once. Without feeling embarassed or apprehensive, I immediately dialled the number and explained my troubles and intentions to a kind lady who called herself Edna. "Come tonight", she insisted quietly, "just ask for Edna. Use only your first name; it's much easier that way." I liked the anonymity: if they weren't going to ask my name, neither would they pester me with questions concerning my occupation, where I lived, my family. I placed all my hopes on this meeting. The telephone conversation had pleased me and I was anxious to go to the address indicated. I imagined it to be a center offering medical, social, psychological and recreational services, group therapy and what not. I had made a firm resolve: to follow their therapy to the letter without discussing or questioning anything they asked me to do.

Not being familiar with the address, I got there late. A few people had already arrived and were listening to a man talking. I sat down quietly and paid scant attention to what was being said, because it seemed to have to do with some point or other concerning the Association which didn't have anything to do with me. I regretted having arrived late. I should have liked to talk to Edna, ask her questions about the therapy and about many other things I was eager to find out. Glancing curiously at the walls, I immediately noticed a large wooden board on which was engraved the following: "These are the twelve steps we have gone through and which we suggest as a programme for recovery." What luck! I had found the object of my search: the recovery programme, therapy! I continued reading: "We admitted we were powerless over alcohol—that our lives had become unmanageable." This first step fitted me like a glove. The following, however, spoke of God, of moral inventory, prayer and meditation. I can't find words to express my disappointment. I read and reread; I couln't believe it, and I muttered to myself: "How can people talk like this after the struggle we have just gone through." I felt completely exploited. I had fallen into a well-laid trap of ignorant, unbalanced moralists and religious nutcases. To my great confusion, the first speaker—I was so upset that I didn't remember a word he said—was followed by a judge, two lawyers, a nurse and a millionaire business man, from what I could gather. I could not understand that the police had not yet closed down this racket. However, although I didn't agree with their way of thinking, I was drawn to the people present who were undeniably very nice and friendly. Reassured by their kindness, I calmed down and realized that I could express my doubts, even my complete disagreement with their "twelve step" programme, filled with religious gimmicks.

I went back a few times to visit with that group. They had suggested that I should not worry about the twelve steps for the time being: it was not a *sine qua non* condition and, if I so wished, I could tackle that later. Furthermore, they assured me that it was not about religion or anything of the kind. If one day I felt like it, I could turn to a Supreme Power, or God, as I understood Him. This clarification satisfied me, and since I was left completely free, I willingly conceded that certain people could find comfort in prayer—on condition it wasn't imposed on me.

How shall I explain my refusal to accept spiritual values? I certainly wasn't an atheist. Moreover, I would not even have taken a stand on the question, because at that time I was totally indifferent to it. My problem lay elsewhere: I knew for sure that it wasn't up to God to deal with the problems of alcoholics. I agreed that alcoholism was a disease and I reasoned thus: if you have a liver disease, you don't entrust your liver to God's care, but to a liver specialist. The same applied, in my humble opinion, to a raging tooth ache: far better to go to a dentist than to church. Alcoholism, I believed, was more apt to be cured by psychology than prayer and meditation. My attitude was in no way motivated by a feeling of resentment against the clergy, or by the hatred of God. I merely considered it idiotic to pray when I could find a cure. At an A.A. day-meeting held at Fort Lauzon, I remember a woman named Betty explaining that only a spiritual experience had brought her an answer to her problem of alcoholism. Had I not considered Betty as an intelligent, educated person, I would have paid little attention to what she had to say. But, knowing her, I felt obliged to reflect on her statement. Besides, she claimed that A.A. had proven its worth. Their group, the first one in Quebec, was spreading rapidly, and most of its members, now abstainers, had shaken off their obsession with drinking, not to mention the hundreds of thousands of other A.A.'s throughout the world who benefited from the programme. That's when I came to this conclusion: neither Betty nor any of the others were true alcoholics. Had they been, I reasoned, they could never have abstained for so long on a spiritual programme alone, without having recourse to science. But I acknowledged that I was a true alcoholic. Hence, I needed serious, sustained scientific help. I ended up being the only alcoholic among all the members of A.A. at Fort Lauzon. I had always admitted "being an alcoholic", but that never stopped me from drinking.

Just what was wrong with me? I lacked "poverty of spirit." When I came to A.A., I was "rich". I am not talking about money, of course. Do you remember a quotation from the Bible which we often heard in our youth: "Blessed are the poor in spirit for theirs is the Kingdom." To be rich in spirit is to be so full of one's own personal ideas that there is no room for the ideas of others. We had also been taught "If you wish to receive, you must first empty your cup". You cannot pour anything into a full cup: that was obvious enough. Each one of us is a cup: you reading this book, I who am writing it. And "Jacques's cup" then was full of himself. Full of my illusions, my certainties, my self-discovered truths. I was completely turned inward, drawing only on my inner riches. My credo was: "I believe in me, in what I say, in what I think..." If that wasn't pride! Which doesn't mean that I was unpleasant, rude or offensive.

Outwardly, I respected the opinions of others, or at least I refrained from openly contradicting them. But inside, I held to my way of thinking. Moreover, I was sincere, which incidentally increased my distance from others. I was "rich" of such wealth that it barred me from entering the Kingdom.

Since the recovery program at A.A. held little interest for me, I spent my time there chatting with other members, smoking cigarettes and drinking coffee. I felt as alone there as I had always been with friends at a bar or at a party with one hundred and fifty guests. Totally bored with these meetings, I stopped attending.

But it was with regret that I dropped Alcoholics Anonymous. Many of the people there were very endearing, like Betty, with whom I had talked a great deal, and others whose names I have forgotten. I envied what they had achieved: many felt happy and even claimed to be free from the urge to drink. But far from convincing me, their claims merely strengthened my conviction that they had never been alcoholics; they had merely indulged in too much liquor, and having family obligations, they abstained from alcohol for the sake of their loved ones. In fact, most of them were married, had raised children; in other words, they had devoted their lives to someone, whereas I lived for myself alone. Besides, I deemed they were all "good" enough to have the right to include God in their lives. Not I. I had long believed that I had placed myself beyond the bounds of God's love. It is important to understand that I did not refuse the spiritual programme of recovery because of either resentment towards my teachers or animosity towards God.

In the course of the years I spent in college, I had indeed met a few narrow-minded professors or supervisors, but I never equated their words about God with God Himself. However, one concept had made a profound impression on me: one had to "deserve" God's love. To get close to Him, one had to be worthy of His love, renounce Satan, his works and all his vanities. Moreover, one had to keep all the commandments, and be in a state of grace; in other words, lead a holy life. This would earn us the privilege to receive Holy Communion, and to bask in the good graces of God and our professors.

Coming back to this God was far too demanding for me! I felt I could in no way comply with the requirements. At no time did I blame God for my lack of courage; I was the unworthy one, though heaven knows I should have loved to bring about the reconciliation! In New York, where I was living at the time, I became so desperately alone and isolated that I wrote to one of my friends in Montreal, suggesting that perhaps a spiritual experience could help me, to which she replied: "If you believe a spiritual approach can help, by all means grab it; it's your last hope." But before receiving her answer, I had already changed my mind. God would not accept me! God's love, the Lord's tender mercies were for honest people, good people who did their duty by Him. My sorrow was real; I felt rejected by the Lord Himself! But it wasn't the Good Shepherd's fault—I had nothing against him—it was all my fault: through my fault, my own most grievous fault. I believe it is at that point that I stopped loving myself and others. I lost all hope. My downfall was catastrophic. In New York, however, not living with people capable of spirituality, I was not inclined to make comparisons. But with A.A. members, decent people whom God loved in return, I felt out of place. And so it is with a lingering nostalgia that I had stopped going to A.A. meetings.

My attempts at abstinence had taught me that I was even more unhappy when not drinking than when I was drinking. It's terrible, but true. My entire social life was geared to meeting my friends at the tavern, then later at a club where we drank until dawn. These were post-war days; masses of people piled into these night clubs where we carried on pretty wildly. You could meet interesting people there: some had travelled widely; others were musicians, artists or writers. We would often meet at a concert or a lecture before going on to a night club. Alcoholics are not by definition uncultured morons. We had fun and enjoyed each others' company; some of those bonds of friendship have lasted to this day.

But when my "obsession" for abstinence took hold of me, I would stay at home and mope, or would meet my friends and stick to soft drinks with cherries or slices of lemon. Have you ever had ten or twelve in a row? Try it. Alcohol is a much better stimulant than these, believe me.

Though it meant going to the clinic once or twice a year, I much preferred drinking heavily and enjoying life to staying home, rambling on about how happier I would be without alcohol. During all those years, I always felt a lot more miserable and lonely when I didn't drink. So I inevitably went back to drinking. I would have had to overcome alcohol altogether... A.A. didn't offer me "victory" over alcohol; it offered to liberate me. Something entirely different!

The years went by; my isolation deepened while my wish to end it all grew. I decided to sell everything and settle in New York where I could more easily live without alcohol. There was so much to do there: concerts, the theatre, museums, exhibitions... I could find enough distractions to keep me from getting bored! I ended up by going only to the neighbourhood bars, nowhere else!

As I spoke of my alcohol problem to everyone, people recommended this psychiatrist who specialized in alcoholism. Her solution was the same: total abstinence. So was the result: the usual fiasco. I decided to move to Paris. Much as I loved the city, French culture and the elegance of the Champs-Élysées did not solve my problem. Understanding my helplessness, two of my friends, Bob and his wife Marjorie, invited me to come and live in Dayton, Ohio. I liked the city, met interesting people, didn't drink and felt neither alone nor unhappy. Three days later, I came home minus a jacket, a tie, a wallet... dead drunk!

Is there any point in mentioning Düsseldorf, where I stayed with one of my brothers, and where I consulted more specialists? Or Chicago, Columbus, Cleveland, Akron, Cincinnati! Should I speak of the clinics: Roy-Rousseau, Domrémy, Albert-Prévost? Of the hospitals: Royal Victoria, Saint-Sacrement, Jeffrey-Hales, Hôtel-Dieu? Of all the psychologists and psychiatrists I consulted? Of all the conversations I had with my brothers, my sister, my friends? Of the calls, the hopes, the disillusions, the failures, the new beginnings, the promises, the remorse, the discouragement, the troubles, the insomnia, the nausea, the wish to commit suicide, the fears, the anguish, the waiting rooms... and the eleven years it all lasted?

I can never express the extent of my gratitude to all the specialists who tried to help me. They offered me respect and sympathy. I remember in particular a psychiatrist at the Royal Victoria Hospital who wanted to help me so badly that he begged me not to drink, and with so much feeling that I pitied him. I who had never abstained long enough from alcohol to even embark on any serious treatment.

So, after all these years, I decided to give up the fight against alcohol: I was just going to drink, come what may. It was then that some members of my family, totally dismayed and fearing that I might come to harm, arranged to have me placed in a psychiatric asylum for a period of one year. I was thirty-three years old; still young. I knew I was not stupid. But the loneliness and inner isolation had finally had the best of me and I agreed to internment.

Part two

BLESSED ARE THE POOR
IN SPIRIT, FOR THEIRS
IS THE KINGDOM OF HEAVEN

Came to believe that a Power greater than ourselves
could restore us to sanity.
Big Book

I was not unhappy at the psychiatric centre where we were treated like royalty. Excellent food, a spotlessly clean hospital run by nuns, the unfailing courtesy of the personnel, all played a part in making our stay there very pleasant.

A few days after my arrival at Saint-Michel-Archange, my family's decision on my behalf was made known to me. I was resting when I was called to the parlor. A stranger presented me with legal papers with the solemnity of one issuing a summons. A Court Order was placing me in custody for one year. I know I shall surprise you, but I could not understand how illogical it was of my family not to intern me for life. From my past experience, I knew that one month, or ten years for that matter, made little difference. On being released, I was convinced that I would go back to drinking.

The weeks went by. Having recovered from my tremors, I ate like a horse and slept fourteen hours a day. However, the idea of spending a whole year in this hospital bothered me. I knew the solution was not to be found here. I had to find something else. But what? For ten years, I had mulled over that very question; now I was desperate.

At this point, I began going over my life. As a child, as a teenager, my dreams, like yours, had been to become somebody! I believe that wanting recognition as a person is a basic need of every human being. It is not the result of pride, but a legitimate ambition. Do you know any young lawyer who seeks anonymity? Every young medical doctor hopes to become not only competent, but well-known, even famous. The most humble of servants hopes that his services will be recognized and procure his advancement. In short, becoming somebody is relative, but it always represents the hope of reaching the top.

Becoming somebody for me meant many things; my problem was deciding which of these was most important to achieve my goal. Why not try them all? Money, prestige, education, travelling and all that entails: luxury cars, elegant furniture, big receptions... How was I going to get all this? I didn't worry about it. I dreamed the dreams of youth! Would that I were a multimillionaire! How generous I would be! My generosity would attract attention and love. Oh yes! I would buy love, admiration, understanding and kindness. All those who came in contact with me would experience joy; I would be somebody! Somebody wonderful, fantastic, extraordinary! But alas, in reality, I was shut up in a hospital, alone and broke, in bleak despair, calling on death to deliver me.

On a wall in my room, a little calendar carried a picture of a Jew with long hair and a beard: the God of my childhood. It was a reproduction of a famous painting by Warner Sallman, not of the suffering God, but of Christ with a kind, serene face. I don't mean to impose this particular God, but that face appealed to me. It awakened in me feelings of love, acceptance, kindness and forgiveness, suffering and understanding. A long-forgotten quotation came back to me: "I stand at the door and knock, and if someone opens, I shall enter and make my home there."

In one moment, I had the revelation that beyond this Face, I would find all the peace, the consolation, and the loving compassion of which I had so often dreamed! I understood that I would have to make an act of faith and commit myself completely to this Face or I would be lost for ever: "I have come to save those who are lost!" I felt unworthy, but I had just come to understand that His compassion was far greater than my unworthiness, that His love reached far beyond my transgressions, and that His kindness could melt my heart of stone. I burst into tears before such infinite goodness. All became clear: with Him, I would find the courage to be happy; with Him, it would be easy to stop drinking; with Him all was possible. And I began to talk with Him, non-stop, telling Him how unhappy I had been, but now that was all over since He was there; that I placed all my trust in Him; that He would teach me, guide me; that we would be friends forever! And I made Him a promise: "If you do something for me, I shall bear witness to it." That promise I have kept, and He knows with what love and gratitude! Exhausted by the intense emotional experience I had just lived, I lay on my bed to rest, convinced that one chapter in my life was finished and another was about to begin.

I had barely closed my eyes when someone knocked at my door. The person to whom I called to enter half-opened the door and stood in the hall to talk to me. I remember nothing of his physical appearance. He spoke to me in English: "I noticed that you were reading in English in the dining room; I thought that you might enjoy reading this novel. I am leaving the hospital; my wife is waiting for me. Keep this book; it is yours." And before I had time to utter a syllable, he put the book on the table near the door and disappeared.

I got up to get this "novel", the title of which was "Alcoholics Anonymous"! My reaction was instantaneous; even before beginning to read, I had already given assent to what the book contained and made the decision to join Alcoholics Anonymous a second time. I scanned the table of contents and found a chapter on "How it works". I began to read: "Rarely have we seen a person fail who has thoroughly followed our path." Reading on, I came upon the twelve steps of A.A. The same steps which ten years previously had put me off:

1. We admitted we were powerless over alcohol—that our lives had become unmanageable.

2. Came to believe that a Power greater than ourselves could restore us to sanity.

3. Made a decision to turn our will and our lives over to the care of God *as we understood Him*.

No words can describe my deep joy at having found what I had hoped for! These first three steps of Alcoholic Anonymous, I had just gone through them! And, in a moment of recollection, I remembered: "Happy are the poor, for the Kingdom is theirs". I had become "poor".

It was as simple as two plus two. I was now absolutely convinced that the spiritual programme of A.A. was tailor-made for my needs. I would commit myself to follow their way; this time, I would not fail. I phoned my family and explained, on the one hand, my hopes with A.A., and on the other, the futility of stagnating in the hospital for a whole year. The superintendent of the pavilion, Sister Saint-Bernard, whom I wish to thank very sincerely for her services, shared my belief. My family, a few days later, signed the papers necessary for my release from the hospital.

Meanwhile, one of my brothers who numbered some A.A. members among his clients, suggested that they visit me in the hospital while I waited for my discharge. I remember the name of only one of these men: Louis. Our meeting was short but very friendly. They had come to encourage me to persist in the decision I had made, and I was touched by their concern. I met Louis but a few times during my years at A.A., and I take this opportunity to express my gratitude for his devotion as well as the generosity of the gentleman who accompanied him. My heartfelt thanks!

Finally the day I was to be discharged arrived. I had formed no particular attachments at the hospital, with the exception of the person in the room next to mine, whose sharp wit had greatly amused me. We called him big John. But I had realized at once that, in spite of his gaiety, this tall distinguished man, had he not held back, would have cried like a baby. I remember his sad expression when he heard I was leaving the hospital. Distractions are few in these clinics, and it is always hard to part from a pal you could talk to. Going to my room, I said a prayer for him. John would later be the first person I sponsored at A.A. As my taxi sped away, I looked back for a last glimpse of the Saint-Michel-Archange Hospital. I knew I would never go back. Tears of gratitude welled up to my eyes as I murmured: "My God, I thank You."

Nineteen years have elapsed since then. I have never taken another glass of alcohol and have never lived in the fear of starting to drink again... because I have never been thirsty again.

This experience, although very hard to bear, was a revelation which confirmed one of the most important paragraphs in the *Big Book* of A.A.: "Once more, an alcoholic, at certain times in his life, has no effective means to mentally control the urge for that first glass. Neither he nor any other human being, except in rare cases, can help him. His protection can only come from a Superior Being."

The above is one spiritual experience among many others: "How I came to believe." However, my way is not necessarily yours; there are many, many other types of poverty, other limits, other ways of meeting God.

An important question must be asked: why did I come back to the God of my childhood? The starting point was, no doubt, that I had heard of Him at home, at school, everywhere. Besides, someone raised in North America would not have known any other. This stems from a cultural phenomenon: the West being at the time predominantly Christian, most religious denominations centred their beliefs around Christ. It is difficult to imagine anyone born and educated in Canada or the U.S.A., forty or fifty years ago, adopting Buddhism or Islamism wholeheartedly. When it happened, it was always an isolated case. Even if Marxism and Oriental philosophies have exerted some influence in North America since then, the fact remains that, in 1981, Christianity still held first place. However, if one were to believe in Christ merely because one had been told of Him, it would be less faith in Him than in those who spoke of Him. Furthermore, what were we told about Him? Did we have a true picture of Him?

In Whom or in What do you believe? What are your reasons for remaining faithful to the God of your childhood, or for having strayed away from Him? The answers to these fundamental questions cannot be overlooked if we wish to embark on a spiritual journey. I shall endeavor to write about "a Supreme Being" within the cultural and social context that is ours. My purpose is not at all to impose, but rather to present one way of following the Alcoholics Anonymous steps: the way I chose, and which I had the good fortune to explore. But it is important to remember that, with its twelve steps, A.A. proposes a programme of spiritual awakening based on the experience of men and women everywhere who have suffered, and whose sufferings have led them to God. Which means that the A.A. programme is not just theory but is deeply rooted in human experience. That is why the A.A. steps are not unlike, in practice, what Paul or the good thief on the cross might have lived; both of these, as each of us no doubt, travelled the road to Damascus. In fact, anyone who, failing to find help, consolation or relief, has known such suffering that he turned to God, has already lived through the first three steps of A.A. And if his experience is authentic, he will search his soul, examine his past, his present and his future. If he has encountered the God of love, his hatred will give way to compassion. This God of love will challenge him to surpass himself, that is to forgive and make amends for any wrongdoing. God will have become his Life, his point of reference, his guide, his confidant; dialogue and prayer will ensue. And because an authentic encounter with God necessarily (by philosophical necessity) involves a change, those around him will want to know what has happened; he shall bear witness. Saint Paul behaved no differently, and the good thief, had he lived, would have done the same. It follows that the originality of the A.A. programme has to do with structure, and not with substance.

The Search for a Supreme Being

This search is nothing new: it has been going on since the beginning of time! Primitive man, incapable of explaining natural phenomena, believed that thunder was the voice of an angry god. God of fear, the Greeks will call him Zeus, and the Romans, Jupiter. Everywhere altars were erected to gods out of fear or interest. Never out of love. Man prayed to the gods for rain, or a good hunt; he offered sacrifices, often human sacrifices, to appease their wrath. But the gods always had the better of him; such was the destiny of man. Thousands of gods sprang from man's mind, more and more gods: stars, animals, men and women—kings and queens, emperors and pharaohs—mountains, rocks and volcanoes. Each one has a God as he conceives Him to be. Closer to our times, the Hurons, the Algonquins, the Iroquois and the Apaches will also turn to God as they conceive Him to be. Sometimes, gods are built: totems or a golden calf. As if their many gods were not enough, the ever-imaginative Greeks and Romans invented demi-gods—and why not?—making a creative use of the entire cosmos:

the Sun, the Moon, Jupiter, and so many others. Gods of the sea and of the wind, gods of war, of harvest... The more gods, the merrier. The cruellest gods, it must be said, were the human gods. That should not come as a surprise, because whenever a man substitutes for God, he only substitutes his power and, tragically, becomes a despot. The Pharaohs enslaved hundreds of thousands of men because they believed they were superior to them. When man makes himself God, his foolishness reaches divine proportions. When man makes himself God—and that's quite a reach!—he loses his humanity. I much prefer a God who becomes man—what a comedown, but what humanity!

Art and literature, science and technology have not made our world much more enlightened; we still have our golden calves: cars, furs, diamonds, comfort, prestige, sex, travel... "Happy are they, who like Ulysses, made a nice journey..." When you come to think of it, we are not much further ahead than the Greeks or the Romans. Perhaps even worse off: the gods have disappeared; we have kept only the travelling!

It's clearly commonplace to say that, from the earliest times, men everywhere prayed to "God as they understood Him." This quest for the divine honours rather than discredits them. Aware that they themselves were not the authors of nature, and wishing to find a meaning for their existence, they turned to something, they did not quite know what, or whom. What else could they do but turn to a God as they understood Him? Such is the humility of man who suffers, hopes and waits.

In the light of all this, let us now consider how the proposition of a "Supreme Being", or "God as we understood Him" is viewed by Alcoholics Anonymous. We must clearly differentiate between Alcoholics

47

Anonymous as an Association, which enunciated the twelve principles of A.A., and its members. These are two separate and distinct realities, and it is essential not to confuse one with the other.

First of all, why is the verb "understood" in the past tense? Does A.A. suggest that its members revert to the God of their childhood? Not at all. The past tense has a historic value, since the twelve steps literally tell a story: the story of "how" the first members of A.A. managed to overcome alcoholism. It is precisely the "how" that saved them, and they decided to pass it on to us in the form of twelve basic principles. At the time these principles were formulated, the founders and their friends had been free from alcohol for several years. Therefore, the A.A. steps provide an answer to the following question: "How did you set yourself free from alcohol?" The answer could be something along these lines: "At the beginning, a few years ago, we decided to commit ourselves to God as we understood Him **at that time**." This cannot be emphasized enough: God is as we conceived Him "at that moment" when we completed step three. It's quite possible that this God was indeed the God of our childhood, but not necessarily so.

"God as we understood Him" connotes freedom, peace, reassurance. It is this very notion of freedom that has allowed A.A. to offer its services in hundreds of countries with different cultures, ideologies, religions, beliefs. This freedom as to the choice of a Supreme Being is fundamental to A.A., and a powerful expression of its acceptance, understanding and respect for each individual. And that is why the association will not introduce a specific God to its members. The late Bill W., founder of A.A., declared: "The degree to which an alcoholic will succeed in placing himself in the hands of

God is not the affair of A.A. Whether it be in a church or not, in this particular church or in that one, it does not concern A.A." Bill is referring to the vertical structure of A.A., i.e. the world services in New York, the general services offered in every main city in the world, the inter-community groups in these cities, as well as all the other official services providing literature and information to the public.

In fact, if someone were to phone world services in New York to find out "who" or "what" God is for Alcoholics Anonymous, he would likely be told that A.A. is non-denominational, and that each member must, in a personal quest, determine what he considers to be the Supreme Being.

However, A.A. has also a horizontal dimension, one on the level of individuals, whose role consists in "adjusting" the A.A. steps according to the rhythm, the aspirations, the milieu, education and personal beliefs of each one: I am speaking of Sponsorship. After a certain time, members may ask a person of their choice to act as their sponsor. Others, but this is much less frequent, will not seek an individual sponsor, but will prefer to be helped by several persons. Individual sponsorship, by far the more successful of these two practices, is much more common. One way or the other, new members will raise questions, air their concerns and ask for clarifications on the twelve steps. At this more personal level, the answers provided by individual members do not commit the association as such, its sole purpose being to develop and formulate, in its literature, more general solutions, applicable to all, never specific, at least not on the question of God.

Wishing to complete step two and to reach "God as they understand Him", very often A.A. members will choose a God of their own making. This stems from a good heart and the firm intention of following the programme faithfully. These members generally have a sponsor to whom they confide that they have found God. And that is settled! Questions are not asked because of the personal nature of our belief in God, and for fear of encroaching upon such a fundamental freedom. I agree that someone's personal idea of God is as good as someone else's. In the beginnings of A.A., this freedom led to the strangest choices. One A.A. member in New York, seeing that a bus had "power" vastly superior to his, decided to call this vehicle his "All-Powerful Being". One would want to help such people! I know this case is an exception, but I have often heard it said: "If a cement block serves your purpose, by all means use it..." What is meant is not literally a "cement block", but that anything you choose can be considered as God.

This way of thinking—which is definitely not that of A.A., as we shall see—gave rise to many gods. For some, God is the cosmos; for others, a Force. Others still will say that God is something "electronic"! When asked: "Who is God according to you?", some will answer by saying "where" He is: "He is within me" or "God is the other before me". There is truth in these two statements, but do we know why? Or are we merely repeating what we have heard, without understanding? At A.A., we also hear that "God is Love", which is true. But do we realize that we are speaking of a God who revealed Himself? The God we came to know on our mother's knee? The God of the founders of Alcoholics Anonymous?

To prevent too much confusion, A.A. added twelve precepts to the twelve steps. These are known to A.A. members as the twelve traditions. I shall not discuss them all, but will refer to them when I feel they can clarify what I have to say. The second tradition is useful at this point:

"For the benefit of our group, there exists but one ultimate authority—a **God of love** as expressed in the conscience of our group. Our leaders are but faithful servants, they do not rule."

This tradition relates to the smooth working of the groups, and I don't think it is useful for me to discuss it in detail. But the expression "God of Love" stands out. Is it that easy to find a "God of Love"? Could it be that others before us have found Him, and that we speak of Him out of habit? And, as was said above, we have been brought up in a mostly Christian society: family, school, tradition, all taught us that Jesus was a God of Love. That is no doubt why a large number of A.A. members conceive of their God as Jesus Christ. Is that a "personal choice"? Or did we "inherit" that belief?

The following is a fragment of an authentic conversation:

— Who is God for you?

— Well... He is everywhere.

— I'm not asking where He is, but who He is?

— It's difficult... He is love.

— How do you know He is Love? You didn't discover that on your own: you were told that God is Love. Why do you believe what you were told?

— I don't know... but I know God exists...

— I know that too, but who is God for you? Who is this God of Love?

— I can't describe Him, or give Him a name...

— Doesn't the God of your childhood, Christ, Jesus, appeal to you?

— Oh, yes, He does! Don't you believe in Him?

— Yes, Christ is God as I understand Him.

— Then, why ask me about God if you know who He is?

— I know for myself. I wanted to know what you thought.

— As far back as I can remember, God has been Jesus for me.

— Why didn't you say so?

— I don't know... I didn't think of it... silly, isn'it?

— You see, it's very simple. The next time someone asks you: "Who is God for you?", you can answer that it is Jesus.

— You are right, it is very simple!

The question of God is an extremely complicated one. Sometimes, you have to talk a long time with someone before you find out why he is confused. I am sponsor for an A.A. member who is married to a charming woman and has two children. He is intelligent, very successful in business, generally at peace with himself. His one problem is finding his own concept of God. I was dumfounded when he mentioned it to me. I can't quite believe that he is being entirely serious.

— But, Peter, we have spent years together. I am your sponsor, and we have so often spoken of Christ at great length. Don't you believe in Him?

— Of course I do. But you say that Christ is "your" God. If that is so, then I must find "my own" God!

I could not have anticipated this kind of mental block in a man I consider very intelligent. You should see Peter today, proud to have his God within.

But do we really make a personal choice? What reasons do we have to believe that this God, Jesus Christ, is better than the God another member of A.A.

might simply have conjured up in his head? In other words, are all gods the same? If your answer is yes, then I understand your random choice. However, if your child needs a doctor, do you choose one at random? In marriage, will any woman do? For your home, any house? For your future, any profession? Yet you are free to make a choice in all these cases. Similarly, your freedom to choose a God, "as you understand Him", does not excuse you from searching honestly and earnestly.

In this search for God, I believe it is essential that we examine in depth any religious education we have been exposed to in the past, to see if the "God we were taught" was more forbidding than loving. I have no intention of being critical of our educators, at least not of their intentions: they merely transmitted what they themselves had received—I want to believe it—and they did so in good faith, giving of themselves in the process. But it cannot be denied that our religious upbringing, and often those who had been entrusted with it, have left us a bitter legacy. To make matters worse, education as a whole was in the hands of religious communities. It followed that any injustice suffered was associated with religion. One should not, of course, identify religious educators with the religion itself, but in practice, that is difficult to do. I agree that God should be dissociated from the people who speak of Him, but on the other hand, when the generals give the wrong orders, it's the army we blame for losing. When in boarding schools, children were homesick, it was understandable. But when they were afraid all the time, under constant supervision, continually punished, literally forced to eat food which made them vomit; made to kneel, with their arms stretched out at the sides for hours, humiliated for peccadillos, thrown into hell for foolish things, deprived of their monthly outing for having talked in line; forbidden to attend one of the four film showings a year for some insignificant reason; harassed and stifled, troubled about the mystery of their sexuality because everything about it was shameful, frightful, guilt-laden; fed a non-stop diet of prayers, Masses, Vespers, Benedictions of the Blessed Sacrament, rosaries, obligatory retreats; when, during meals, as silence was the rule, they had to listen to someone read to them in a drone a text meant for fifty-year-old men; when we know that they will not remember a single kind word, so rare a thing it was, one is justified in wondering what kind of religion was in these educators' hearts. Call it a misunderstood religion if you will, but, at the time, through our educators, the only one we knew.

But all that is in the past! How much more open and closer to the true spirit of religion are the priests and brothers of today! Two weeks ago, I went to visit an Ursuline friend of mine in Stanstead. Marie-Bertha is principal of a high school where I saw young people going up and down the stairs, happily chatting without being overly boisterous, a bit unruly but not wild. I stayed in the school for a few hours and sensed all the freedom within the discipline required, an atmosphere of both cheerfulness and self-restrain, of joy rather that fear. Everything was clean and in order. I was introduced to a few nuns, intelligent and serene women, totally fulfilled. In such a school, I felt my love of teaching coming back to me. I have taught in public schools and I sincerely believe that they eventually will have to model themselves after these religious institutions. They have the right formula.

However—and this is sad indeed—many are those who will not, or cannot, forget an early education full of prohibitions and taboos. Not having been, for a good number of years, in contact with nuns or brothers, they cannot see for themselves how much they have changed. Yes, the Church has changed. The Church has changed as much as we have. Can you believe that! Everything has changed. Are you one of those who have been left behind? Whatever the case may be, I often wonder in what way the message of Christ was proclaimed if so many people today can feel liberated only when they stop speaking His name! And if, in an attempt to help them in their search for God, I bring up the Lord Jesus of their childhood, they will be quick to react:

— Don't talk to me about any of that! is a frequent response.

Their aggressive tone reveals deep wounds. Total shutdown! Yet, if we love them, we must help them journey back to the past—to console, appease, comfort them — and listen to them. And so, I go on talking, gently questioning:

— Why do you refuse to talk about religion?

The answers are always the same:

— Because I'm not interested! Brothers, sisters, priests: they're all crackpots. They never understood us, much less listened to us! All crackpots, I tell you. The hell they preached!... let them all go there! Everything was sinful, ugly, shameful! You think I'm exaggerating?... No thanks! Find yourself another sucker for their God!

This is but a fraction of what I hear, and I have left out the cursing. But, as they are not taking it out on me, I go on talking, showing that I understand them:

— I understand all that! All you say is true. You have talked about priests, sisters, and hell... But you haven't talked about Jesus "the Jew", whom you knew in your childhood. What do you have against Him?

Right away, there is a softening in the tone.

— Him? I don't have anything against Him.

— If you wish, I always say, I should like to talk about Him. But, mind you, after our chat, If He doesn't mean anything to you, just forget the whole thing. But I don't approve of your rejecting the God of your childhood out of "resentment" toward priests and nuns.

I hope that everyone understands how illogical it is to reject the God of our childhood simply out of "resentment" toward those who made Him known to us. It's an aberration! That someone I sponsor should refuse to accept the Christ of his childhood doesn't bother me at all, provided he does it for logical reasons. And to be in a position to do so, he must first "know" what he is rejecting. It's not an easy task, for it means returning to the past and starting our religious education from square one. We must get to know the God of our childhood, not by listening to those who first spoke of Him, but by listening to His message. Only after having done this will we be able to decide. But before studying more closely the message of Jesus of Nazareth, and reflecting on the reasons for believing in Him, I should like to touch upon the question of God.

The Question of God

In the first place, is it childish or naive to believe in God? You have no doubt heard, as I have, that only stupid, ignorant people can possibly believe in God, people whose ideas have not evolved in keeping with our modern world. Some, upon hearing that you believe in God, will merely smile, because they love you and do not wish to hurt your feelings. Such an attitude would indicate that Pierre Teilhard de Chardin, for all his genius, was really a simpleton, as must have been Pascal, Bach, the Maritains, Marc Oraison and thousands of other great minds, but otherwise slightly "cracked".

However, that these great minds should have believed in God is no proof of his existence; other great men did not believe in God, many among them geniuses themselves. Hence, let's not be overawed by the assertion that believing in God is childish and irrational, but rather, let us remember that many great men believed in God.

In the second place: do you have faith? Careful now: to believe that God exists is not faith. It is part of the process leading to faith, but you are not there yet. He who admits to the existence of God is closer to faith than an atheist. However, faith is not a belief "in the existence" of God. To have faith is to believe "in" God. And that is something else altogether. If you say that you believe "in" your husband or "in" your wife, you are saying that you trust them. To "believe in" God is to trust Him. It becomes a question of relationship. The belief in the existence of God is merely a statement of your position, and has no direct bearing on your life. But to put yourself in the hands of God out of trust could very well mean a resurrection for you. Can we, in all truth, have complete trust in someone, commit ourselves to him or her completely, unless it be someone we love and who loves us? The founders of A.A. know this: they speak of "a God of Love" (Second Tradition) to whose care we entrust our life (Third Step). We are not lending our car; we are trusting someone with "our life", placing ourselves in His hands; and that is something! But it isn't all: we must further trust Him with "our will". What that involves, we shall look into more closely.

It is easy to place our lives in God's hands if He acts according to "our" will. As a matter of fact, it turns out to be a very good deal: God being all-powerful, it's certainly a line worth developing! And that's exactly what we do: "My God, please do this or that for me, so I won't lose my house, that I may find love, have a car, not suffer or die..." Rarely do we say with all our heart: "Thy Will be done!" Yet, if there is a level on which God and man meet, it is on the level of the will. I would say that God's will and man's will are so much alike that they are one: man is seeking happiness with all his might, and God wants nothing other than happiness for man. But what spoils everything, in our way of thinking, is that God is not of the same mind as we are as to the choice of means to achieve our happiness! We seek to improve our lives through money, comfort, passionate love, prestige, power and glory, wheras God sees progress for us in the detachment from all things! Therein lies our resistance to His Will, does it not?

But there is more, much more to it: we fear God's will. This fear is acquired, that is to say, it was instilled in us. If a child died, what the mother was told was: "Come, my dear, you must resign yourself to God's will", when she needed to hear something like: "I am grieving with you; I understand your sorrow; God will help you to overcome this ordeal...", instead of implying God's "special intervention" every time catastrophe strikes!

Jean-Luc Hétu, wishing to establish a link between the Gospel and psychology, writes in his wonderful book: "If I am obsessed by my need for security, I am bound to consider every event in my life as a providential intervention on the part of God! On the other hand, if I am racked with guilt, I shall interpret all my misfortunes as punishments from God."

The problem of evil in the world is complicated enough as it is, raises enough questions about God, without having to drag Him into everything that happens. If anyone wished to make us hate God, that would be the best way to proceed. A fire? God's will! A car accident? God's will! No harvest? God's will! Mother of eight children dies? God's will! On the other hand: You won a million dollar? Chance was on your side! That is how—for one million—we miss a good opportunity to make people love God! You say: "It would have awakened interest rather than love." So be it! But at least it would have been cause for rejoycing. Always to show God in a bad light is not exactly the best way to bring people to love Him. No wonder so many A.A. members are afraid to allow God to act in their stead. "I have enough trouble right now—they think—without God getting into the act!" I meet lots of people who are seeking a spiritual path and I know what I am talking about: we are afraid of God. His will for each one of us is in the order of mystery, and it's not up to just about anyone to reveal it to us. It is part of God's plan of love for us, a plan which, because of the problem of suffering here below, is far from being clear. God's will is that we should be happy, "in spite of"...: in spite of our solitude and isolation, in spite of the lack of love and understanding, in spite of illness and old age.. "Blessed are the poor... those who weep..." To accept God's will, one must be absolutely convinced of His love. Then will disappear the need for explanations, which are nothing but attempts to justify God. Instead, we shall feel the need to commit to God with total abandon.

Who is God for you? What profound reasons motivated your choice? Are the different concepts of God equally valid?

Gods of stone, gods of iron, primitive gods of early man, gods of the Egyptians, of the Greeks and the Romans, gods of fire: a flash in the pan, all of them, no longer worshiped! All the Gods we invent, imagine, create, gods we pull out of our own heads, the God of Christians—Son of Man and Son of God—Jesus of Nazareth: are all these gods the same? The answer to this question is found in our turning to God—man's quest—or in God's coming to us—God's Plan!

Although philosophy does not distinguish between "idea" and "concept"—it very often uses one for the other—I should like to make a fine distinction between the two. The "idea" of God is the same for all: a Supreme Being, Beginning and End of all things, the Author of Nature, Creative Intelligence of all that is. But "concept"—the way each person conceives God to be—implies a movement, a search to fulfil certain needs which in turn will justify the specific form the idea will take. For example, the idea of a car is the same whether it be a Rolls Royce or a Volkswagen: a chassis on wheels, with an engine. Yet the form each of these two carmakers will give its product is very different, since Rolls-Royce and Volkswagen aim at meeting different needs: prestige, refinement and elegance on one hand, simplicity and economy on the other.

A search—"going towards"—is also an attempt to fulfil a need: I look for a pencil to fulfil the need I have to write; for an apple to satisfy my hunger. To search for God, to seek Him, is also an activity that fulfils needs, an answer to a call from deep within ourselves. What is this call? What is this need so great that man can only satisfy it in a Supreme Being? Isn't there more to fulfil than the need to explain the universe, something our intellect requires? What about the aspirations of our heart? Who will fulfil these? Because man admits that he is not the beginning and the end of all things, has he ever been happier, more understood, more consoled, felt more wanted?

The heart of man longs desperately to love and to be loved, craves for tenderness, understanding, kindness and compassion. Even if your marriage is a success and your children bring you comfort and affection, you still feel that, in the very depths of your soul, there is a lonely place, a part of you no one has touched. There, you are homesick, tormented by the melancholy of exiles far from home, the nostalgia for Paradise lost!

There is also a love that suffocates: possessive love, dependent love, demanding love; these kinds of love aim at fusion, destroy the individual. "Fusion" love would possess the other, keep him within, present at all times! True love demands that each retain his own identity. It is a love "side by side" in which the solitude of one walks arm in arm with the solitude of the other, and the joy of one is reflected on the face of the other; in which suffering is met with warmth and heart-hardness gives way to forgiveness. To achieve such a love, one must first find one's center within oneself. That we should wish ardently to meet someone is most natural. But that life itself should depend on it is too much! If your happiness, the richness of your existence depend entirely on the other, then you are in great danger: should the other disappear, you would be lost, ruined.

But how much lonelier are those who so want to love and find no one! Hearts forsaken, hearts who cling, hearts who wait, hearts so tired of searching that they have given up hope! I do not envy those who find consolation in human love; it is a rare occurrence and a beautiful thing to contemplate. But—and I may be mistaken—I doubt that many alcoholics can ever find in it the total fulfilment of their need to be loved. And I am not at all convinced that anything will completely heal the wounds caused by our deepest feelings of solitude. It is possible to anaesthetize them, with trips, friends, love, television, work, even self-sacrifice, and so many other ways! But we are bound to remain dissatisfied. I believe that we can escape our isolation when we finally accept it. But human beings seems incapable of true acceptance; at best, they resign themselves to their situation. And far from bringing joy, resignation leads to a nostalgia which in turn will need to be deadened artificially. Only the Love of God can lead us to accept our solitude, to consent to live with it, to realize that it will always be with us. Solitude is inherent to the human condition. God does not fill the void so that we shall not cease turning to others. And even in our relationship with God, we must accept a degree of solitude: a perfect union with Him is not of this world. In marriage, as in friendship, it is necessary to accept our own solitude, to realize that it will always be there, and that it is futile to hope that it will ever be entirely overcome. Only then can we begin to live "with" the other, and stop wanting to live "of" the other. The Gospel invites us to give our lives "for" our neighbour, and not to expect life "from" our neighbour. So many people seek their happiness "in the other". They need the presence of others, when in fact love is all about bringing "our presence" to others, "our happiness" to others. It doesn't work in reverse. I hear many unhappy people confide to me that they are alone, and cannot find the will to go on living if they do not find a kindred soul. **He** is totally miserable alone, **she** is desperate to find someone. Both are convinced that there cannot be any happiness without a mate. Suppose they meet each other. What can they give each other but their void? What can they share but their unhappiness?

Each one must find "within oneself" the source of life, the balm for one's wounds, the strength to accept one's limits, a measure of happiness, simple and yet hard to explain, because it stems from a Mysterious Presence, urging us to go on **believing** in spite of everything, **hoping** in spite of everything, **loving** in spite of everything. Only then will our love relationships have a chance to last.

But what is love? It is hard to define, because you can't point a finger at it. No one has ever seen love having a conversation with kindness on some street corner. Neither is it a person like Jeannette, André, Thérèse or Albert. You can't hold love in your arms. That is doubtlessly why so many people are disappointed. Perhaps love is what you didn't find in the person you just left, that same person you once held tightly in your arms. Why didn't it last? "Oh, she didn't understand me... he was never there... she was sometimes harsh with me... he never sent me flowers." Yet it is the same beautiful woman, the same handsome man. Clearly, you can't hold love in your arms. Love is precisely what was missing between them: acceptance, kindness, understanding, forgiveness, security, peace and harmony, patience, humility, gentleness..., all that we long for deep in our hearts. First, love has to be tested in everyday living. Then we can take in our arms this person whom we are now ready to accept as part of our family, forever, with all his or her limitations. But, these very limitations are at the root of that feeling we have of not being loved enough, of not being accepted or understood completely; hence the ever present nostalgia of a more satisfying, absolute love! No one can love us as God does. If someone who could were to be found, he too would be God. For God is Love!

Our impoverished relationships are due to our own limits: we are not capable of loving the other to the point of responding completely to his need of being accepted, understood, loved; we are not God. Our suffering comes from our inability to love as perfectly as gods. And the persons to whom we have commited ourselves are not capable of it either. Which means that, when we look for true love, for the perfect love that will touch us deeply by satisfying our yearning to love and to be loved, what we are unconsciously seeking in our misery is God himself. Provided God is Love.

It bears repeating that an encounter with the God of Love is not easy to arrange. For example, if I tell an alcoholic: "Put God in your life, otherwise you will go back to drinking", I am merely stating a truth borne out time and again in the A.A. experience. But that amounts to a form of manipulation, because I am imposing God with a simple "believe or die". I am leading the alcoholic to God for him to merit his sobriety and avoid a relapse, much as one would attempt to merit Heaven and avoid Hell. God of interest and of fear. It is better by far to give the newcomer "an urge for God". It comes easily to all of us when we find in Him the welcome, the compassion and understanding which we need so much.

But what kind of God is man capable of inventing? A god that reflects his own delusions of grandeur. Suppose you and I invented a god; where would we place him, and what would he look like? We would put him where the people in high places of our own are: on a throne. He would look like our tycoons, living in the lap of luxury, surrounded by servants groveling before them. We would bow to His Greatness, to His Majesty, overcome by the Power and the Glory! In our childhood, we knew this Almighty and All-Powerful God only too well! As for His love, we were supposed to deserve it, so that only great saints—a chosen few—seemed worthy of it.

We should have been taught that love has nothing to do with merit, but is a fundamental need; true love is gratuitous and cannot be deserved. However, the notion of love as freely given is difficult for us to grasp: human beings do not live comfortably with the notion of unmotivated love. Tell a woman: "I love you and I want to marry you" and she will immediately say "Why?" And you had better have some very good reasons to give her! She wants to "deserve" your love. And the more reasons you give for loving her, the happier she will be and the more you will please her ego, since you will make her feel worthy of your love. And don't make the mistake of telling her that she has nothing in particular "to merit your love", because you run the risk of having your face slapped, or her walking right out on you. Besides, you could not love her "for no particular reason". Being human yourself, you do not know absolutely gratuitous love. We act in exactly the same way with God, and believe that He acts in the same fashion towards us: we think that sometimes He loves us, and sometimes He doesn't, depending on whether our behavior is good or bad. We thus submit to a whole ritual in order to regain God's love, while making sure we don't err too often, since God's forgiveness might get a little shaky; moreover, being a bit suspicious, He might lump us together with the hypocrites and repeat offenders. As if God suffered from emotional instability! If God were to cease to love—even the most hardened criminal—for one second only, He would cease to be God, because God is Love. It isn't God who doesn't love the criminal; it is the criminal who won't give God a chance to love him. We shall often come back to this idea, because it is at the heart of this book.

Love is not a question of "merit" but one of "need". Let us suppose that one of your well-liked, devoted friends turns up at a reception you are giving. Almost all your guests know him, and his arrival is greeted with joy. Everybody likes him because he is nice. Ten minutes later, your brother-in-law, or an aggressive cousin, sweeps into your house like a whirlwind; he is a loud-mouth, and he brashly insinuates that you are all just a bunch of snobs, and if he so wished, he could tell some juicy stories! His entrance causes neither joy nor sympathy. The first guest is clearly more likeable and more appreciated. However, which of these two guests needs to be listened to, welcomed, understood, loved the most? Isn't it the second one, ignorant as he is of the ways of love? Of course, our hearts know this instinctively; but are we capable of living according to our hearts?

Let us imagine that you have three children: the youngest is in a serious accident, and he will have to spend the rest of his life in a wheel chair. As the father or the mother of these children, you are very concerned. The mother is prepared to give up the twelve thousand dollars swimming pool she had planned, and to set aside the amount for the crippled child. Most likely, you, the father will hesitate to play golf every Saturday as you did in the past. Because of the needs of the child, you will not be able to dispose as freely of your time as previously; you will want to take the child to the park or to the zoo; in short, you will have to give him more time... Right? The older children may grumble that you are paying too much attention to the youngest. You will tell them that you love them all equally but that the youngest is in "greater need" of your care. Now, what is the reason for this preference? Why the "special love and care"? Certainly not because the child is more intelligent, nicer, or "more deserving" but because he is disabled, "deficient" in one respect. Remember the word "deficient". When we will be called to make the inventory of our moral life, we shall be asked to list our disabilities or "deficiencies". And it will be good then to remember that the more "deficiencies" we have, the more "disabled" we are, the more the Father will lean over us "with a special tender love" because our "need" will be greater. Love is not a question "of greater merit", it has to do with the heart!

Is this how God loves us? Kindly and compassionately as a father and a mother? Absolutely, and even more! If God does not fulfil our profound need to be loved, understood, made secure, taken care of, comforted and forgiven, then I wonder why we would bother with Him. One might just as well turn to that "someone", anyone who could answer our needs. Don't you think so?

How should we go about finding a God who fulfils our basic need to be loved? There is of course Jesus of Nazareth; but what reasons do we have for believing that this weak man who, after all, was put to death, represents a concept of God better than any other? This question has been asked many times in this book and we shall now attempt to answer it. To begin with, let us make clear the difference between a superficial answer and a serious, reflective one.

Incomplete answers and superficial ones come from the intellect—or the intelligence—and being only partial, insufficient, they give rise to fear and anxiety, precisely because they fail to answer what is being asked. I shall explain this shortly. On the other hand, answers which bring calm, peace and security are those that come from our "life experiences".

Let me illustrate this by means of a dialogue. Since you are well acquainted with the problem of alcoholism, we shall suppose that Mrs. Moore—who doesn't know anything about A.A., Al-Anon or alcoholism in general —wishes to confide in her neighbour and friend, Mrs. Taylor. Mrs. Moore has a problem which is causing her "great fear and much anguish", because she has no first-hand experience of this problem. Her son, Ken, who is married and a father of three, drinks like a fish! According to her, he was influenced by that stupid Albert, and she doesn't know where to turn to get her son out of the clutches of "vice". His wife, a real saint, can't take it anymore! Mrs. Moore, who has always kept secret her son's "shameful conduct", can no longer remain silent and confides in her dear, kind friend, Mrs. Taylor.

— Mrs. Taylor, began Mrs. Moore, I will tell you a secret, but you must promise not to reveal it to anyone?

— What is it, my dear Mrs. Moore? Of course, I promise!

— It has to do with my son Ken... He drinks... you know... he has lost his job... no one has seen him in the last four days... it's terrible" (She bursts into tears).

— Good Heavens! Mrs. Moore. What are you going to do? How well I understand you! If I were you, I would lose my mind! I can hardly believe it! Dear Lord!

What I want you to grasp here is the tone of "anguish, fear and shame" arising from the fact that neither of these two women belong to A.A. and thus, having no first-hand knowledge, no experience, they cannot discuss an alcohol problem with calm and confidence. Neither of them is competent to talk in depth about something which they approach superficially on the level of "what they see". Their minds interpret events at face value: without a doubt, an alcohol problem in a family of five is no cause for rejoicing; it is indeed very serious, but that is all they know about it.

Now, let's suppose that Mrs. Moore had confided in a friend who was also a member of Alcoholics Anonymous. In the first place, she would not have been so afraid to talk about her problem, knowing that this friend would be able to provide her with answers from "experience". And indeed, the friend's response would have been reassuring and soothing:

— Why, yes, Mrs. Moore... I had an idea that your Ken had an alcohol problem. But he is not alone, you know... take me for example... There is great hope, Mrs. Moore. Maybe your son would be willing to meet me...

As you see, the A.A. friend has a tone altogether different from that of the neighbour. He "knows" how serious the problem is—who could know better?—but he also knows how to solve it. His first-hand experience gives weight to what he has to say.

That is because personal "experience" is at the very level of "being". By the level of "being", I literally mean the level of the verb "to be": I am, you are, he is, etc... This A.A. friend of Mrs. Moore's "is" a reformed alcoholic; he "knows" what he is talking about! To be able to talk about something "in depth", it is better to "be" that of which one talks. No one can talk about medicine as well as someone who "is" a doctor; no one can explain the technical problems of playing the piano as well as a pianist. If one "is" neither a doctor nor a pianist, it would be well to refer to their opinions to talk about medicine or piano technique. Otherwise, we may be talking nonsense. That seems obvious enough: I would rather consult a plumber for plumbing problems that a ballerina! We may logically conclude that, just as a plumber talks best about plumbing because he "is" a plumber, the one best able to talk about alcoholism "is" an alcoholic.

No wonder that men—"not being God"—say so many foolish things about Him! Some great minds—like Plato and Aristotle—had a more rational approach, much closer to the truth. But generally, people said just about anything: "He is the Sun", or "He is the Pharaoh"; "He is Caesar", proclaimed the Romans.

As for the Jews, their knowledge of God came directly through revelation. Yahweh had spoken to their prophets, of whom the most famous were Abraham and Moses. But the coming of Christ revealed God more clearly and more precisely as Love, something that had remained hidden up until then. Who could talk better about God than God Himsel? Which brings us straight to the following point: what if God had come in our midst? What if, seeing our misery and suffering, He had decided to bring us a message: the "Word" of Consolation and Acceptance? If God had come to breathe the air we breathe, to share our humble joys and sorrows, if God had come to talk to us about God, surely He would have known what He was talking about, since He "is" God! "The Word was made flesh and dwelt among us".

Let us pause on the WORD. By "word", we must understand "message". The word is the message. And the word—or message—is the person. It's not "like" the person; it "is" the person. For example, Bill W., founder of Alcoholics Anonymous, was bound to die, to disappear as a man. But his message—the twelve steps capable of reforming alcoholics—keeps his memory alive among us. That Bill W. had grey hair and green eyes... that he lived in the State of Ohio are interesting facts, but they add nothing in themselves. For the message, the word, is the spirit. The spirit does not die as long as there is someone to transmit the message. Bill W. is more present, more alive today than he ever was during his life. Why? Because more and more A.A. groups were formed over the years, and this has allowed many more members to benefit from the message. Bill is hence present for a greater number of persons. The message, the word, is the person.

God has placed us in one of his grandest and most wonderful creations: all of nature! Everything about it speaks of power, order, harmony and beauty. But when I say that God alone can speak well about God, I am referring to the Revelation of a God who loves us as a Father, as tenderly as a mother, of a God capable of loving us beyond our wildest dreams! And then, of course, there is the God of the philosophers... but: "He who is from the earth belongs to the earth and uses earthly speech. He who comes from heaven bears witness to what he has seen and heard..." (Jn. 3:31-31).

Take a clock, look at it, take it apart, put it back together: it will tell you of the skill of the clockmaker, but it will reveal nothing more on the man himself. But, should this clockmaker knock at your door and spend three years with you, you would have a wonderful opportunity for getting to know him. That is exactly what God did in the person of Jesus of Nazareth. Christ is God become incarnate—a Man—in order to speak to men in a human language, the only one they can understand. "No one comes to the Father except by me. If you knew me you would know my Father too... He who has seen me has seen the Father" (Jn. 14:6-9). Finally, it is certain that if God became Man, it was not only to bring us a message; it was also to redeem us with his Death and to merit Eternal Life for us. However, what I wish to dwell on is the "message" rather than the mystery of Redemption.

The God of Bill and Bob

Who was the God of Bill and Bob, the founders of Alcoholics Anonymous? The answer should not be difficult for anyone who knows the facts. Bill and Bob were both American; and the majority of Americans are Christians. This may come as a surprise, but in my many conversations, I have discovered that people very often do not know the meaning of the word "Christian". The word comes from the Latin "Christianus" whose root is "Christ", and means related to Christ. Catholics are not the only ones to believe in Christ; other denominations, like the many protestant sects, also profess faith in Him. In the United States—home of Bill and Bob—Catholics and Protestants speak of *The Lord* with the same relig-

72

ious respect. Bill was a Protestant and Bob a Roman Catholic; hence their God was the Lord Jesus Christ. But that in itself does not tell us if Bill and Bob remained faithful to this way of seeing God. They could have changed over the course of the years. However, if you have ever attended a single meeting of A.A.—on the condition that it was presided over in the most widely used tradition—you will have doubtless recognized the God as conceived by the founders. In fact, tradition would have it that each meeting of A.A. should come to a close with the reciting of the Our Father, the same prayer that Jesus taught his disciples when they asked Him how to pray (Lk. 11:1).

To make sure that this closing prayer was not due to some over-zealous Christian member, I resolved to find out whether Bill and Bob recited it themselves when they presided over their meetings. If such were the case, then the tradition dated back to the founders. I approached Dave B., founder of Alcoholics Anonymous in Canada. Dave had certainly seen and heard Bill W. preside over meetings of A.A. in New York or elsewhere. Dave told me that Bill would always bring the meeting to a close by saying: "Those who so wish may join me in reciting the Our Father."

This is a clear indication that Bill W., founder of A.A., believed in Christ, and consequently, that his concept of God was Christ *The Lord*, but that he would not impose his belief on others, and thus allowed the members complete freedom in joining or not joining him in reciting the Our Father. He did not impose his religious views, but neither did he hide them.

The preceding paragraph has profound implications for a Christian. We like to say that the founders, Bill and Bob, were men inspired by God. If the founders, in the third step, placed themselves in the hands of God, it was in the hands of the Lord Jesus Christ, and were therefore inspired by Christ. Which amounts to saying that Christ, through Bill and Bob, founded Alcoholics Anonymous in 1935. This last assertion holds no difficulty for Christians who recall some of Jesus' last words: "And he assured them, I am with you always, to the end of time." (Mt. 28:20)

God and the Commandments

A daily event, a chance encounter may transmit a Word, a Message from Jesus. What does He bring us that is new and original? Does He come to remind us vehemently of the commandments? Must we look upon Jesus as a moralist, in the strict sense of the word? I don't think so. We don't need to be religious to know that we must not kill, must not steal; any decent man or woman bows to these laws; they are a matter of course. It's natural law, but Christ has added a new and original dimension to it , namely that God is Love. If you know that God is Love, then you must have learned it on your mother's knees, and you must have grown up in Western society, which is greatly influenced by Christianity. If A.A. members talk of a God of Love, it is because their founders were themselves imbued with Christianity. Christian morality is above all one of Love. The distinguishing characteristic of early Christians was that they loved one another.

Jesus recognizes and respects the Law or the commandments, but He teaches us about Someone much greater, much more important than the commandments. That Someone, greater than the commandments, is God

Himself, the God of Love and Forgiveness. God's message to the world is that even if we have sinned, even if we have broken the Law, as long as we admit it and turn to the God of Love, we are forgiven and always loved by Him. God is Love. If God is Love, He is all-forgiving.

Forgiveness, you see, is the exact measure of love. You can never fully know that you are loved as long as you haven't been forgiven. That someone should offer you a mink coat, or whatever other expensive gift, in no way proves he loves you. Do you want to know if someone loves you? Play a dirty trick on him. If he slams the door in your face, you will know. But if he forgives you, what do you conclude? That he loves you. And the greater the offense, the greater the love that forgives. Forgiveness is the yardstick of love. That may be the reason why we allow ourselves to be harsh with those who love us: on the strength of their love, we are sure of their forgiveness. We are always polite and courteous with people whose esteem we are afraid to lose. But with husbands, wives, parents, we are less careful: we know things will straighten themselves out in time.

As we all know, twenty-five or thirty years ago, the Church did not exactly welcome fringe groups with open arms, and that goes for alcoholics. As a result—and such was my case—these groups distanced themselves from the Church and all religious practices. Not necessarily out of resentment, but because alcoholism is very problematic on the moral level, and also because life as an alcoholic and the requirements of religion are completely incompatible. Many of us, for some fifteen or twenty years, paid scant attention to the evolution of religious thought, so that some still believe that the Church has not evolved much either. And that is a great

75

pity. The passing years always bring some suffering, and with it comes change. If the years have wrought a change in us, they have done so in the Church as well. Yes, the Church has changed.

Whatever the case may be, let us cast an eye on the past. The time has come for us to see if Jesus' message had something to say to us alcoholics. Something to do with Love. To do so, we must contemplate the life of Jesus; but beforehand, let us consider briefly our early education, the mentality of the times, the climate in which we were brought up.

Compared to today's approach with young people, our education was narrow-minded indeed; this is true everywhere in the world. Does that mean that we are raising better men and women? I am not at all sure, but I don't intend to enter a debate on the question. One thing is certain, however: no educational system is perfect.

It may be useful here to mention the significant influence that Jansenism had on our culture, with its strict definition of morality, as well as that of Puritanism, mostly in New England, to whom we owe, among other things, the exaggerated modesty in dress that was required of women before World War II broke out. I distinctly remember seeing, at the St. Louis-de-Gonzague boarding school, in the 1940's, a stern warning, posted at the entrance, that women with sleeves above the elbow would not be admitted. I hasten to add that the nuns in charge were intelligent, very amiable, certainly not crazy! It seems that, at the time, the essence of morality and the very quality of a human being were entirely focused on modesty of dress, and consequently on sexual behaviour, of which no one dared speak openly, so shameful and out-of-place a subject it was. A woman who dyed her hair was looked upon with suspicion: a bleached blonde was considered to be a sinner, as if natural brunettes were ice-cold! A woman wearing slacks to church created a scandal. All infractions against modesty were reported to the teacher, the parish priest, the Mother Superior, all of whom made sure everyone heard about it in order to protect the innocent. The mind boggled at the thought of divorce, and only people of considerable means could even contemplate such a move in the face of universal disapproval. Fortunately, the war contributed to broadening the outlook of an entire generation. However, if views on fashion were being liberalized, the whole question of sex remained taboo for several years to come.

Education in the 40's also stressed prayer, attending Mass, the obligation to abstain from meat on Fridays, performance of one's Easter duties, scrupulous payment of tithes, and abiding by other similar precepts which do not reflect the essential message of Christ's Love. Finally, those who were exposed to life in a boarding school will remember the emphasis placed on rules, to such a point that talking in line was considered a venial sin. "To talk back" to a teacher would have been sheer madness; we would never have dared!

I must add, however, that I am not against the above-mentioned principles. I would have wished more flexibility and subtlety, that's all. But I want to draw your attention to the fact that I cannot remember having been told that God accepted us, and loved us just as we were, and that His love would help us to become better persons. Furthermore, rarely, if ever, did our teachers validate our behaviour: we were never told that we were good children, gentle and submissive; our patience, our efforts, our perseverance to be what we were asked were never even acknowledged; only our failings were pointed out. We had to be taught our place. Our educators were lucky to have children like us: we were angels! I should like to see them teaching in colleges today.

These remarks on the narrow outlook of our past education were not meant to level reproaches at anyone. I am not trying to dramatize, or to imply that we suffered the same fate as Jane Eyre or David Copperfield at the hands of our educators. On the contrary, on many aspects, I prefer by far the kind of education I received to the one being offered now, especially as far as discipline and the teaching of academic subjects are concerned. No one can deny that our teachers, who worked for one hundred and fifty dollars a year, were very devoted and gave all their time and energy to their students. We worked very hard, our progress was closely followed, and we obtained good results.

What I deplore is that everything which had to do with religion—and hence with God—was always negative, depressing, and left a bitter taste. The first ones to suffer were the teachers themselves; they must have felt suffocated by their religious principles as much as we did, if not more. God's presence in one's life brought no joy, no freshness, no sense of liberation, no kindness, no rest, no respite. Far from teaching us to lavish love and acceptance on others as well as on ourselves, this poorly understood religion seemed, more often than not, an invitation to pass judgement, condemn, scorn and cause pain. That is surprising when we listen to the words of Christ: "Judge not and you shall not be judged" (Mt. 7:1), and: "I have spoken thus to you, so that my joy may be in you, and your joy complete" (Jn 15:11).

The only explanation for this misguided way of thinking is that we had failed to understand Jesus' message, and that the New Testament had not superseded the Old: our mentality was still that of the old Temple of Jerusalem: the narrow-mindedness and lack of compassion of those who taught there had provoked Jesus' indignation. What shocked Christ was not so much to see Mary Magdalene's buttocks, but rather all the scheming that went on in the higher realms of power, the influence of money over justice, the exploitation of the poor by the rich, the lack of love. And what frightens me is the thought that, if Christ came back today among us and denounced the same injustices, taking sides with the weak against the strong, the Blacks against the Whites, the poor against the rich, the exploited against the exploiters, He would be so quickly executed, in secret and without a trial, that His death would barely be mentioned on the evening news. It is much easier of course to attack Mary Magdalene than the powers that be. The Evil that Jesus came to fight against was the spirit of Satan, and the spirit of Satan is also the spirit of Mammon, that is to say money and the power it can buy. People kill for money, exploit for money, pretend to love for money, refuse to give to the poor for money, lie for money. Engineered political trials, assassinations by proxy, false information, manipulation of the masses are all motivated by power and money. The spirit of Satan is far more international than individual. That leaves us with Mary Magdalene. Without approving of her sinful life, Christ forgave her right away and didn't make a big fuss about it.

Our religious education needs a complete overhaul. For example, nothing is more beautiful or more true than the story of Adam and Eve, of the apple and the serpent, provided one does not stop there, but goes beyond the symbols of the tree and the serpent to discover that each one of us too one day, took a bite of the apple. The Lord had given man to understand that he could dispose of all he saw, that Nature was his to enjoy. However, God was to add, human beings did not have the necessary insight to determine what was good or bad for them, or where lay their true fulfilment and genuine happiness. God had therefore admonished them "not to eat the fruit of the tree of Knowledge", in other words not to "bite" into the idea that we didn't need His help in deciding our destiny; otherwise, we were heading for disaster. But in creating man free, God took the risk that His children would refuse to obey, to remain with Him and to entrust their happiness to their Father. This freedom is almost unfortunate; one would wish that we had been created without it. But God is Love, and where there is no freedom, there is no love. Do you want to know if your dog loves you? Undo his leash. (It is this notion of freedom that gives rise to the problem of evil in the world.) The value of the statement: "I am staying with you" is in the right to say: "I won't stay, I am leaving." Similarly, what gives value to meekness is the privilege of being able to get angry. If that were impossible, wherein would lie the virtue of the meek? If we were not free to close our door to the poor, what merit would there be in opening it? We would inherit the kingdom of sheep! And so, to go on with our story, an insidious idea literally snaked its way into the mind and heart of Eve (it could very well have happened to Adam... but the story was written by men): "Well now, look here, God... it's time we did something about this: we're not idiots! Enough pious nonsense! We are perfectly capable of making our own decisions and running our own lives."

Does that remind you of anybody? It reminds me of the time I decided to take control of my own life; I would, on my own, find happiness; just wait and see! I didn't need God. Besides, it would be a lot easier without Him.

And finally Eve succeeded in convincing Adam. Clearly this means that the majority agreed. I don't believe that only one man and one woman were involved. Jacques Cartier is supposed to have been the first European to stand on Canadian soil. That doesn't mean that he was alone when he did it! Once they had made the decision to run their own lives, the strong enslaved the weak and put them to work. People started to hate one another, to kill one another. Love ceased to exist. In the beginning, men were conscious of God's presence in their lives. They lived by, through, in, for, with God. Separating from God is tantamount to separating from love, harmony, acceptance and tenderness.

This awareness of God as part of one's life, once lost, is difficult to find again. Ask lovers who have broken off their relationship how easy it is to make up! Having strayed from the path which leads to the heart of God, we have been thrown into a world devoid of love. Because he had not yet tested his limits, man was as pretentious as a teenager who leaves home and who, when asked to return, cries out: "No, never. I don't need anybody!" For God did call Adam and Eve: He asked them what was going on, what they had eaten that didn't agree with them! But their conceit, their pride prevented them from seeing His love. Instead of expressing regret, they made excuses: "I didn't do it. Eve did... it isn't I, it's the serpent..." (It isn't my fault, it's my wife's... I'm not responsible, society is...). They say that if Adam and Eve had answered: "We are sorry", the face of the world would have been changed. But we can't hold it against

Adam and Eve: how long did it take you to say: "My God, I'm sorry?" And how much longer, do you think, will it take for all nations, all governments, all mighty leaders to look up to heaven and say: "We are sorry"? I would rather not think about it!

The story of Paradise Lost is that of man in search of complete autonomy, God being in the eyes of man a form of "alienation" or a kind of "opium for the people". Later Christ would tell us about the unfortunate experience of a lost Paradise. He would invite us back to it in the parable of the prodigal son in which he tells us that the door was never closed, that it is still open, and our Father is there waiting for us, his arms wide open. What's our excuse now? In the meantime, we shall have to conquer human folly. That will take some time!

And then there were angels and devils that made quite an impression on us: beautiful angels, with their great feather wings, and hairy devils who terrified us, with their horns and claws on their hands and feet, not to mention their amazing tails! I do not wish to elaborate on the world of angels and demons, but we must admit that there exist in us both good and evil tendencies; our kindness reveals our angel side, our meanness, the devil in us. We could also call angels all those messengers, our true friends, who always wished us well, and devils those who enticed us to place our hopes for happiness in ephemeral and false gods. However, angels have neither wings nor feathers, and demons neither horns nor claws. It was the inimitable Louis Evely who, in one of his lectures, insisting that angels had no feathers, added with humor: "As long as you believe in this heavenly fowl...!" I loved that. But there is nothing silly about representing angels with wings and devils with horns: it merely reflects the artistic sense of another era. The

Middle Ages stressed the visual to a high degree. Is not our modern age characterized by the audio-visual? Artists, painters and sculptors were asked to depict the story of the world from Creation to the Last Judgment. If you had to draw a picture of Good and Evil, you would see that it's not that easy. These two realities do not exist as such (it would be quite something to see Good and Evil walking together down the street), and so artists personified them and gave them a familiar form. Now, one can say of a good man that his thoughts are "noble", that he is of God, hence, from on high. And angels, so graceful on the wing—the "Victory of Samothrace" comes to mind—admirably suggest the nobility and beauty of goodness. On the other hand, a man with horns, some sort of hairy, ugly beast, is an apt representation of the mind of one whose thoughts are said to be vile and abject. But there is a world of difference between symbolic representations of Good and Evil, and literally believing that angels have feathers, or that if you have been bad, a hideous, hairy creature will come at night to grab you by the toes.

This idea of a frightful demon grabbing you by the toes makes you smile, doesn't it? Today's sisters and brothers would smile too. That's all in the past. Today, religion is much more concerned with the Word of Jesus and His way of life as told in the New Testament.

The New Testament takes us right to the Temple. It is there that friction arose between Jesus and the clergy. In Jerusalem, all the activities in the Temple were reserved for nice, decent people, those who followed the Law, Moses' commandments to the letter. Women, not being considered as persons in their own right, were not allowed to speak in the Temple. Do you remember reading: "There were two thousand people, not counting

83

women and children"? Christianity was to become a formidable movement for the liberation of women, especially in those countries where women were obliged by law to keep their faces veiled in public.

Then there were "the others": the sinners who were pointed out as those God pursued in His wrath. For example Job, an erstwhile prosperous man held in respect by all, who, having been gravely ill, lost his fortune and found himself penniless. Job was wont to say that he had sinned grievously, and God in His justice had punished him. Therefore, the sick, the poor, the infirm had no one to blame but themselves, since God was punishing them for their sins! This mentality is still with us. Have you ever been tempted to ask yourself what you had done to deserve some misfortune which had befallen you? Many believe that if they suffer trials, it is because they have done something a bit dubious. Past masters in the art of shaming the unfortunate into guilt, the worthy Temple goers had reproached a blind man with his sins. He defended himself and argued that his blindness could not have been caused by his sins, as he was born blind! They replied that his parents, then, must have sinned very grievously indeed! There was no way out: the blame had to be pinned on someone. And, it goes without saying, God always punished the guilty ones.

But if we look around us, there is no evidence that God punishes the "big sinners". Don't many notorious crooks own villas in Florida or on the French Riviera? And many of them drive a Rolls Royce! Furthermore, if we act merely to avoid punishment, there is little love to be found in our behaviour. We still worship a God of fear and interest. No, God does not punish, nor does He take revenge. I have met many people who, under the pretext of forsaking a Vengeful God—as they call Him —have become estranged from the God of Love of their childhood. Jesus taught us to forgive, not to seek revenge; how can we speak of a Vengeful God? The following text may help to convince you:

> You have been told: "An eye for an eye and a tooth for a tooth." But I say to you: do not set yourself against the man who wrongs you. If someone slaps you, turn the other cheek. If a man wants to sue you for your shirt, let him have your coat as well. You have been told: "Love your neighbour, hate your enemy." But I say to you: "Love your enemies and pray for your persecutors; that way, you will truly be the children of your heavenly Father, who makes his sun rise on the good and the bad alike, and sends rain on the honest and the dishonest. If you love only those who love you, what reward can you expect? Surely the tax-gatherers do as much as that. And if you greet only your brothers, what is so wonderful about that? Even the heathen do as much. You must therefore be perfectly good, just as your heavenly Father is perfectly good." (Mt. 5:38.48)

The perfection of the Father resides in His unconditional love for all men. But man must open his heart freely to that love.

Finally, among those who were poorly thought of at the Temple were thieves, beggars and prostitutes. As for adulterous women—not men—they were liable to death by stoning. Strangely enough, the God-made-Man sided with these people—the beggars, the poor, the sick and the infirm, all those "punished" by God, Mary Magdalene, the adulterous woman—He blasted the Temple goers who relentlessly condemned these poor wretches, calling them "hypocrites", "vipers", "whitened sepulchres." Then turning to the hord of those who had always been rejected and scorned, He declared with a kindness and compassion so deeply touching: "You are the salt of the earth... you are the light of the world!" (Mt. 1:13-14). And that is a great consolation to me. Christ's tender love is so great that it is difficult for us to fathom. A wonderful man—whom I do not have the pleasure of knowing personally—helps us to discover this in his writings: the great Louis Evely. I have read all I could find by this author whom I consider as a spiritual guide, a friend, an "angel" at my side on my journey. A lot of what I have written in this book has been inspired by him. Do read some of his works to see for yourself how extraordinary and profound his thinking is.

There is no getting around it: if we want to have some idea of God, of His Love and His Compassion for us, we must, not only listen to Jesus speak, but also watch Him live his life on earth.

The Infinite Power of God

It is fitting to speak of God as All-Powerful. Just look at the universe. However, Jesus did not hold power to be an important value in itself. If He agreed to perform a few miracles for the unfortunate—always out of love and compassion for their suffering—Jesus did not use His Infinite Power to save Himself. And it stands to reason that, had He held scholarship in esteem, Christ would have made sure that everyone knew Him for the great scholar and philosopher that he was. Why wasn't He born of a wealthy and noble family? Because that would have given too much importance to nobility. Jesus had but one value: Suffering Love.

Have you ever noticed that true love always implies suffering, and always on the side of the one who loves the most? Generally, parents are the ones who suffer the most: they miss their children and complain incessantly that they don't get to see them enough. But the children, preoccupied with their own passing joys, find their parents unreasonable. And so, those who love the most suffer in silence for fear of alienating the objects of their love. Those who love less are more independent, stronger; they can slam doors.

When we happen to see a movie on the life of Jesus, we find ourselves wishing He would defend Himself and finally show those morons who He really is! Deep down, what are we looking for? God the Almighty! It is so hard for us to accept the notion of a God of Love. It took Jesus a much greater Love to refuse to defend Himself and consent to his Supreme Sacrifice. If love means accepting the other with all his limits, Jesus accepted humanity with all its nonsense, its violence, and its unqualified stupidity. That is Love! I have already said that the measure of one's love was forgiveness. In fact, just before committing His soul to the Father, didn't Jesus implore: "Father, forgive them, for they know not what they do." Forgiveness is indeed the true measure of Love.

When we consider a God dying on a cross, we justifiably question His Power. The only answer is that His Love for us rendered Him Powerless. It is always the one who loves the most who allows himself to be crushed.

... and I believe that the passage which describes a dying God resting on His human Mother's knees indicates the lowest point to which a divinity descended, and it is also probably the highest peak reached by humanity (R. Dowling).

I think that if God had not allowed Himself to be put to death by men, we would seek another God of Love. What could we say of Jesus then? That He had put up with us for a while, that He had shared our humanity, our few joys, our many sorrows, even our insolence; but that at some point, He felt we were overdoing it! Then Jesus would have said: "Enough is enough! Carry on yourselves, I'm quitting." God would have shown His Almighty Power! But that would have been a God unable to accept us in all our failings. We would be entitled to expect a far greater love, capable of seeing us through to the bitter end.

If suffering remains a mystery for us, Jesus' suffering can at least give it meaning in our lives. If God's Suffering saved the world, I can at least understand that my own suffering saves me from myself, on the condition that I embrace it. For suffering which is not accepted can destroy us; but if embraced, it will lead us straight into the Kingdom. The Power of God is the Power of Love. Gazing at Christ on the Cross, one realizes how great is man's power over God.

God Came to Serve; He Is at My Service

That God should be at my service is surprising. But how could it be otherwise? How could I serve God? What service could I possibly do Him? God has perfect insight; He alone can help me. When you are in trouble, do you say to God: "I am coming to help you", or "My God, help me"? Now if God helps me, if He is the one doing me a service, then by the same token, He is at my service, is He not? If we have difficulty understanding that God is at our service, it is no doubt because we have discredited the concept of service. To be in someone' service does not mean "to be his slave". Mrs. Menuhim once stated on television that loving is to serve: "I am wholeheartedly in my husband's service," she proudly declared. A real father, a real mother, are at the service of their children, isn't that so? Those who have the most, in whatever capacity, must serve. Is not a teacher in the service of his pupils? Since he has the knowledge, it is he who can serve them. Jesus did more than just serve through His teachings. He became a cook for his friends, knelt to wash their feet, and often adopted with those around him attitudes characteristic of a servant. Finally, could Christ have made it any clearer when He said: "The Son of Man has not come to be served, but to serve" (Mk 11:45). If we wish to serve God, we must serve our brothers and sisters; and indeed, the second tradition of A.A. states: "... our leaders must be faithful servants; they do not rule."

The Colour of Love, the Colours of God

If God is Love, He must sport the colours of love. And what are they? Love is embracing, patient, meek, kind, generous, indulgent, understanding, humble, calm, consistent, gratuitous, tender and so much more. If God is Love, we must expect to find acceptance in Him, tenderness, patience, forgiveness, humility, understanding, meekness, security, generosity, gratuitousness, fidelity, courage, calm, harmony and peace. These are God's colours, His Way of Being, His Way of relating to us. But I must not only "imagine" that this is so; I must be able to experience this Love both in the "message" and in daily events. For instance, it may sound extravagant to say that God is "humble". But I didn't invent that attribute for Him. Jesus Himself said: "... for I am meek and humble of Heart." (Mt. 11:29)

A word of caution: these are "God's" colours! He alone possesses them perfectly, without limits. People have often confided in me: "I am incapable of loving; I find it impossible to accept my husband or my children. I lack kindness, humility, warmth and understanding..." Come now! As far as I know, you are not God! Neither am I! God is Infinite Love, Love without bounds. In Him, the range of colours is therefore limitless. Unfortunately, we are limited. If loving someone means accepting him with all his failings, we are certainly unable to love to that extent. To love ourselves also means to accept ourselves as we are, with our own limits; I believe that we are equally incapable of doing that. God alone can offer total, gratuitous, unconditional Love. We should not feel too sad that we are incapable of such an ideal love. It is already something that we acknowledge our limits. God will help us to grow in that direction.

God is Love. If Love Is Joy, then God Is Joy

"These things I have spoken to you, that my joy may be in you, and that your joy may be complete" (John 15:11). How is it that we so rarely experience perfect joy? The reason is that we seek it outside of God! We search for happiness which, as I have pointed out many times, we always identify with money, love, travelling... It bears repeating, so deeply engrained is the idea that happiness comes from an external source. But let us look at Jesus and listen to His words to see whether He radiated joy.

We know that Christ restored sight to the blind and we marvel at His powers. It's those powers that most impress us. Christ didn't have to heal: if He did so, He was prompted by love and not by a desire to prove His omnipotence. Note that He ceaselessly cautioned his listeners "not to breathe a word to anyone." And the joy experienced by the blind must not be forgotten in the wonder of their cure. It is easy to imagine the delirious joy felt by someone who had been miraculously cured, by his spouse, his children, his father and mother, his brothers and sisters, his friends and the whole neighbourhood!

Christ was constantly overwhelmed by a feeling of compassion for the poor and the wretched: "And when He saw them, he pitied them because they were weary and helpless like sheep without a shepherd" (Mt. 9:36). This is why Jesus had consented to celebrate the feast of the loaves, the fish, and the wine.

In those days, people often went hungry. A large crowd had gathered to hear Jesus speak. When it came time for the midday meal, they noticed that they had but a few loaves of bread and a few fish to feed thousands of people. It is then that Jesus multiplied the loaves and the fish. Do you think that Jesus did this for his own Glory, to reveal His Power, or do you believe that He acted out of love? That is THE question! If God had come down among us to reveal His Power, why did He allow Himself to be nailed on the Cross? All those people ate their fill, and still there was plenty of bread and fish left! People must have been amazed at such abundance. At the time, the common people, living in poverty, had to beg for bread. It was such an important issue that Jesus felt he should include, in the prayer He taught his disciples, the words "... give us this day our daily bread" (Lk. 11:3). It's not unlikely that many among the poor crammed their pockets with bread. And yet, there were enough loaves left to fill twelve baskets. Wonder and Joy must have been the order of the day! What a contrast between God's munificence and man's wretchedness! Yes, what Joy! What Love! God did not want us to see in Him more power than love. That explains his rather sad comment: "... you seek me... because you ate your fill of bread" (Jn 6:26).

Cana was celebrating a wedding and the whole village had been convened to drink, eat, dance and be merry. Was this really something which God should be asked to attend? Wasn't He going to dampen the congregation's spirits by His presence? God is no laughing matter! You don't drink to excess, or have too much fun when He is around. But, since He had been invited, God came to the wedding. And in a way so characteristic of Him, out of love, He changed the water into a wine far superior to the one that had been served first, and far more plentiful. God always gives nothing but the best! However, He didn't like the idea of intervening: "My hour has not yet come", had been His initial response to His Mother. But she wasn't going to let Him get away with it; she knew her Son's heart too well: you could always wear Him down in the end! His Mother said to the servants: "Do whatever He tells you!" (Jn 2:5). And Jesus, torn between the knowledge that "His hour had not yet come" and His desire to please, decided in favour of the latter and changed the water into wine. Of course, everybody was amazed, but how many saw in this miracle a gesture of Love? There again, far from being a spoilsport, God was a source of plenty and of joy. Not the sentimental, exuberant kind that accompanies the acquisition of material goods, but the profound joy we experience at becoming aware of the giver's tender love for us.

In Love's field of force, even the most insignificant everyday event is transformed into joy. To leave this field of warmth, compassion, and joy is tantamount to losing "our conscious link with God himself within ourselves", and as a result, we become sad, worried and aggressive. "Sought through prayer and meditation to improve our conscious contact with God..." (Step 11). It's when we pause to think and pray that we can find calm, peace, and joy again. Only love can give a "sense of joy" to life. Then, any offering made though love becomes true joy, an authentic sacrifice.

That a sacrifice can mean joy may come as a surprise. However, for it to be authentic, and after the manner of God, a sacrifice must bring joy because God is Joy. We were taught that our sacrifices had to have a bitter taste of self-renunciation, and the more agonizing they were, the greater their value. But a sacrifice is an offering, a present; if our presents are accompanied by long faces and contrite attitudes, it is better by far not to give any. Besides, the recipient would feel no joy in accepting such gifts. Let us suppose that your neighbour, a good friend of yours, has been the victim of a vicious assault and is rushed to the hospital; her children have been left in the care of an aunt. You have a key to the house and you go in, only to find it in a mess. Everything needs to be done: the dishes, the beds, the dusting, the vacuuming, the floors, and so on. In a burst of zeal, you say to yourself: "Wait till she comes back; she won't recognize her own house!" You get down to business and spare no effort. You actually do more than is necessary, because you want so much to surprise your friend. You can just see her face when she walks in! You can't wait to see her reaction! You are relishing the thought of her own joy. Nothing can stop you. You run home to get a bite, and you come back refreshed: "Will she ever be happy!" The work itself is no picnic. You can certainly think of nicer things to do than scrubbing floors. But you have known this charming friend for years, and you are very fond of her. When you were ill, and depressed, didn't she take good care of you? It is your love for her that makes scrubbing those floors pleasant. Sacrifice is difficult; in some cases, it may even require heroism on our part; but love will transform it into joy. A.A. members have an extraordinary sense of "giving", of "true sacrifice" offered in love and joy. The day finally arrives when your friend comes home from the hospital. When you see her getting out of the car, you rush to cross the threshold with her; it is the moment of your offering, that of her joy: yours too!

However this love for your neighbour is not in itself sufficient to make of your offering a "sacrifice"; it remains an "offering." In its original sense *sacrum facere*, sacrifice means "to make sacred an ordinary gesture". Atheists are perfectly capable of scrubbing floors out of love for their friends. However, since it remains on the human level, this kind of love and dedication can only make us better human beings. But if, in addition to acting out of love for others, we add another dimension to our love, and act out of love for God, we do more than grow as persons, more than "humanize" ourselves; we will be blessed, "sanctified" and, why not, run the risk of becoming... saints! "A glass of water given in my name..." It all depends on what we mean by "becoming a saint". If we look upon saintliness as something outside of man, so exalted as to be inaccessible, then any notion of attempting to become a saint is unreasonable and extravagant. Do you think St. Francis of Assisi was very different from Mother Teresa? And yet the latter couldn't be more human; we have seen her in the flesh on television. What makes saintliness appear inaccessible is that we picture saints as statues, frozen in time and tradition. In order to humanize the notion, one should read at least one biography of a saint. If you haven't, I recommend very strongly that you do. Nothing is more interesting. As in a television program, or in a good novel, a life will unfold before your very eyes. You will understand the character and get attached to him as a friend; saintliness will become a living, human reality. We naturally cannot all aspire to become Saint Francis of Assisi or Mother Teresa; we are asked only to give to the limit of our potential. Mother Teresa does no more herself; it's God's face she loves in the poor she works for. Love of the poor would be enough to make her a better human being, but through them, it is God's face that she loves, and that makes her a saint. Christianity is a religion of faces! And we can safely say that, in spite of the enormous difficulties she encounters, Mother Teresa's whole life radiates joy!

But there is joy also for another very different type of woman : the adulteress. Had God Himself not been there at the right time, she would have paid with her life for not obeying one of the ten commandments. The law of the Temple demanded that such a woman be stoned to death. There and then, commandments and principles were more important than a human life. This way of thinking made forgiveness—and hence love—impossible, and was bound to meet with Christ's disapproval, since He came as the God of Love and Forgiveness. Now, "the scribes and the Pharisees brought a woman who had been caught in the act of adultery; they brought her before the people and said to Jesus: 'Master, this woman has been caught in the act of adultery. Moses laid down in the Law that her kind should be stoned. What do you say about it?' This they said to Him, that they might have some charge to bring against Him" (Jn 8:3-6). They set a subtle trap for Him; for had Jesus approved of the stoning, He would have contradicted His teaching on love and forgiveness; on the other hand, being against it would have meant contradicting the Law, and that would have placed Him in a difficult position. "As they pressed Him to answer, He stood up and said to them: 'Let him who is without sin among you cast the first stone.'" (Jn 8:7). We know how they all left, one by one, without casting a single stone.

"Let him who is without sin..." Did not this challenge on the part of God make us understand that the sin of adultery, like every other sin, must be viewed with compassion and love, until it dissolves into forgiveness? Could it be that God, far better than we can, is able to plumb the depths of our minds and hearts? In the heart of Mary Magdalen, the heart of the Samaritan woman and the heart of the adulteress, Jesus did not see joy or pleasure; only pain. "Judge not, that you be not judged. For as you judge, so shall you be judged, and the measure you use for others will be used for you." (Mt. 7:1-2). Without God's intervention, everyone, wishing to conform to a religious precept—inconceivable as that may be—would have stoned the woman to death.

It is always dangerous to place principles above people: "The Sabbath was made for man and not man for the Sabbath" (Lk. 2:27). Somebody pointed out to me that in its twelfth tradition, A.A. speaks of placing principles above persons. Certainly not! A.A. wants to place principles above PERSONALITIES, which is not at all the same thing!

What Is God Made of? What Does He Look Like?

It seems that those who surrounded Jesus were preoccupied with the same questions as we are: "What is God made of? What does He look like?" And Jesus would always answer that God looked like a kind, loving Father. He knew that what we needed most was love, and theological dissertations on God's attributes mattered less than knowing whether He was well-disposed towards us. "Tell us more" they would plead. And in an attempt to better describe Him, Jesus, God Himself, had told them of the "Prodigal Son" (Lk 15:11-32).

His father was well-to-do; God the Father, presumably. Jesus couldn't possibly present Him as poor, since God is joy and abundance! "This father had two sons. The youngest went to his father and said: 'Father, please give me my share of our inheritance.' So the father divided his estate and gave him his share. Shortly after, the youngest son gathered his belongings and set out for a faraway country..." He must have been bored, sick and tired of living at home and having to put up with his father. He was going where the action is, in the big city! Isn't he just like us? Haven't we tried just about everything to find happiness outside of God? As sons, we are free; in our story, the father had let his son go. Transposing what happened to our world, the son had no sooner reached the city than he rented a high-priced apartment, bought himself a fancy car, and started spending his evenings in posh nightclubs where he met all the women mentioned in the parable, who finally brought about his ruin. He found himself on the streets, penniless and without a job. To make matters worse, the country was in the throes of a severe economic crisis. (The parable mentions a great famine). It is at this point that Jesus reveals Himself to be an astute psychologist. Jews don't exactly appreciate pork and, as it happens, the prodigal son has to work tending pigs. Finally, he becomes so destitute and sinks so low that he is refused even the carobs that are fed to the pigs. In his bleak despair, he thinks of going back home to the Father. Doesn't that remind you of someone? And don't the words of the text: "Searching in his own heart..." remind you that it is only "within oneself" that one can find God, that real values are found in the "inner self"? However, the prodigal son does not expect to be received and loved as a son. Believing he no longer "deserves" to be loved, he feels unworthy of the Love of the Father. At best, he expects to be treated like a hired hand. Isn't that how many of us have come back to God? Although we deemed ourselves "unworthy", we still took the road back home, albeit with bowed heads and heavy hearts. We were hoping for so little, so very little! Just a little love, a touch of kindness, a shadow of a smile. And if that were asking too much, then only the right to look at the house from afar and see, on special occasions, the windows light up; to catch from a distance familiar sounds, the cherished voices of our childhood. We would have promised never to show ourselves, never to speak, never to ask for anything. And more than that, never to complain, nor to cry; to always be good and perfectly still, if only we were allowed to stay, and wait. For what, we didn't know; we were so desperate!

Maybe a tune from long ago carried on a light breeze. My God, we asked for so little! Then are we really "poor": when, knowing that we have no right to anything, when we don't deserve anything, we manage to find, deep inside, just enough FAITH, just enough HOPE, just enough LOVE to give us the courage to go back home!

"But while he was still at a distance, his father saw him and was moved to compassion; he ran to embrace him, he kissed him and held him in his arms for a long time. The father said to his servants: 'Quickly, fetch the best robe and clothe him with it, put a ring on his finger and shoes on his feet; bring on the fatted calf and kill it; let us eat and make merry; for this is my son who was dead, and he is alive again; he was lost and he is found.' And they began to rejoyce and make merry." You can easily imagine the prodigal son's astonishment. That's because God is never what we had anticipated. God will always surprise us: if He didn't, if He were what we had imagined Him to be, He wouldn't be God. It is God's Love which is beyond us, so beyond us that we cannot imagine it, or what God is.

Now the elder son came back from the fields, and as could be expected, he began complaining about his father's excessive generosity: "... This son of yours has squandered your money with harlots, and yet, when he comes home, you kill the fatted calf!" And the father said: "Son, you are always with me, and all that is mine is yours. But it was only fitting to rejoice and make merry, for your brother was dead and he is alive again; he was lost and is found!" The elder son still couldn't get over his surprise. "I have served you for so many years, never disobeying your command; yet you never gave me a kid that I might have a feast with my friends..."

Now isn't that strange! The faithful son regrets having stayed, and the prodigal one regrets having left. But since leaving home had brought him suffering, the latter was the better off of the two. Suffering always teaches us something; it makes us realize that we are incapable of finding happiness on our own. Fear not, the prodigal son knows that the kingdom is in his father's arms. He has suffered enough to learn that. As for the elder son, he thinks that happiness is a banquet his father has never offered him. He doesn't know yet that the kingdom is living with the father. How difficult it is for us to understand that our happiness lies with God!

Besides, neither of the two sons really knows the father. They perceived him as a man of principle, unyielding, and one with whom you must follow the straight and narrow path. However, to their great surprise, both sons realized that their father was far more broad-minded than they thought. The elder son—as many narrow-minded people—gets angry in the face of his father's weakness. The younger one—as those who have suffered and crave for love—is deeply touched by his father's tenderness. The fact remains that one is loved, but fails to appreciate it, while the other is so impressed that he can't get over it. You see how difficult it is to recognize Love for what it is! Who thought of throwing a party? Not the elder son nor the younger one; neither you nor I would have thought about it! The Father did! God is truly and deeply Acceptance, Kindness, Understanding, Forgiveness, Security, Peace, Quiet, Harmony, Generosity, Gratuitousness, Patience, Fidelity, Meekness, Humility, Strength; He is the Truth, the Way and the Life. Because, you see, God is Love.

But it's up to us to open our hearts to this love, to entrust ourselves to it, so that through it we may become sons and daughters of Light.

Now, how can a God of Love reveal Himself through our group consciousness, more specifically the consciousness of our A.A. groups? What I am about to say is strictly personal, and does not necessarily reflect the position of the A. A. movement. I want that to be very clear. I think that our groups, by their unconditional acceptance of all members, express God's love. There are no prerequisites for becoming a member; all that is required is the wish to stop drinking, otherwise we would be wasting our time. No condition of good moral behaviour needs to be met. The applicant's past has no bearing on his entering the programme, his private life does not concern the group: he will be unconditionally accepted. That always reminds me of the scene on the cross: "And he said: 'Jesus, remember me when you shall be in your kingdom.' And Jesus answered: 'Truly, I say to you, today you will be with me in Paradise.'" (Lk 23: 42) Since both the thief and Jesus died at approximately the same time, I always like to imagine them arriving together in the arms of the Father, One radiant with glory, the other, shrinking behind, not quite believing that he has been forgiven!

Among the A.A. members we meet, some become friends, confidants. Among these we may choose our sponsor, someone in whom we have a greater trust. Someone has doubtlessly confided in you, and while he might have been very much at ease, you sensed nonetheless how difficult it was for him to share certain painful experiences. A slight hesitation, a sigh, tears welling up, mumbled words revealed in the person before you a profound need for understanding, acceptance, consolation, love. What did you do? You tried to offer just that, understanding, acceptance, consolation and love. You used words of encouragement: "Come on, don't waste your time worrying about the past; look to the future. We all love you and we enjoy your presence..." You don't scold, you don't condemn. Does the God you chose welcome you as well as you welcome your friend? Does he love you as fondly as you love others?

Some people do not think God capable of accepting them, of understanding and forgiving them, of making them feel secure with as much fondness as they themselves offer the people they are listening to. And that is a shame. How much greater than ours is God's tenderness for us, how much bigger His Heart, how much more all-encompassing His Love, more humane His Divinity! But, you object, what about divine justice? We are human and we are no doubt more accomodating, inclined to forgive too easily: isn't that indicative of our very humanity? Set your mind at rest! God's humanity is infinitely greater: it was raised to the level of the Divine!

God's Justice, Man's Justice

As for God's justice—and I am certainly glad about it —it has nothing in common with human justice. Let me give you an example: "You did that? Wonderful. You will be rewarded with a medal, an increase in salary, a promotion." Or else: "You are responsible for this? Too bad. Eight days in prison." No chance of a fatted calf! Everything is right, but cold, lucid, legal... and human! However, there is no reason for waxing enthusiastic over such extraordinary, marvellous, transcendant human verdicts. Sorry, I'm sticking to my opinion: I'll take the fatted calf any day!

It has taken millenniums to abolish capital punishment. Until recently, justice demanded an eye for an eye, a tooth for a tooth. After proof of an assassin's guilt was established, he was put to death. The taking of a human life is a serious matter; it is the ultimate injustice to a human being and to those who love him. Hence, the Prosecution had to plead very convincingly to obtain the death penalty for the prisoner. He had to repeat over and over again—and with reason—how grievous an offense killing is, a frightful, terrible, horrible, monstrous deed; then, the prisoner was brought in and he was told: "We are going to kill you!" Struck with the absurdity of this type of reasoning, the law-makers voted the abolition of capital punishment. Others, no doubt sincere and for motives they consider valid, are asking for its reinstatement. I do not wish to enter the debate, having neither the knowledge nor the competence to do so. I am just basing my position on the Word of Love: "You have heard it said: 'An eye for an eye, a tooth for a tooth.' But I say to you..." (Mt. 5:38).

God in His justice neither rewards nor punishes; He always forgives. The only condition is that we open our heart to His Forgiveness, to His Love (God Himself); that is essential. There is no "justice" of God in our sense of the word "justice". The one and only justice of God is the "Justice of Love."

The justice of God "justifies": it places the wicked man on the same level as the righteous one, so that both are invited to the celebration. The justice of God is forgiving. And God can never be accused of injustice because He grants forgiveness to all those who ask for it. To quote once again: "Jesus, remember me when you shall be in your Kingdom" and Jesus answered: "Truly, I say to you, today you will be with me in Paradise". The Kingdom is given gratuitously to all; if the good thief never strayed again, that's because he never had the opportunity! God's justice comes down to this: His love and His forgiveness open wide the doors of the Kingdom to the assassin as well as Saint Theresa of the Child Jesus. Is that injustice? Not at all. Love? Why, of course! And it doesn't take anything away from Saint Theresa. I wouldn't be at all surprised to see the latter engaged in conversation with a notorious criminal. For Theresa can't be jealous—jealousy is a deficiency—and since she shares in the fullness of God's love, she can only forgive.

Those who would be condemned are those who refuse forgiveness, and in so doing, would condemn themselves. God never condemns. But suppose someone refuses to be forgiven, doesn't believe forgiveness is possible? To be able to accept God's forgiveness, one must first believe in God, in His Love. What can God do if we don't want to be saved, if we don't believe in His Love, in His forgiveness? If you want to get God, refuse His forgiveness. He'll be stuck! Remember the Prodigal Son? If he hadn't come back, how could God have thrown a party for him?

There is little doubt that the Parable of the Vineyard was inspired by the jealousy Christ must have sensed among his disciples. This parable is about the owner of a vineyard who hires workers for a denarius a day. The pay of one denarius is a symbol for the Kingdom. Now, some worked all day, others half a day, and some worked barely one hour. Imagine everyone's surprise when, at the end of the day, everyone, without distinction, received full pay, the sum of one denarius that had been agreed upon! God will never fail to surprise us! His justice is entirely different from ours: don't forget to "punch in"! The owner of the vineyard heard the usual complaints: "The workers hired last only worked one hour, and yet they got the same treatment as we who have borne the burden of the day and the scorching heat." But the master replied to one of them: "Friend, I am doing you no wrong; did we not settle on a denarius? Take what belongs to you and go; I choose to give to the last workers as much as I give to you. Am I not allowed to do what I choose with what belongs to me? Must you be jealous because I am generous?" And so the last shall be first, and the first shall be last (Mt 20-13-16). God's justice does not stop at being "fair"; it goes far beyond in a surge of kindness: it is "the Justice of Love".

Does That Mean We Can Do Anything at All?

Does that mean that we can do anything at all? If we are always going to be forgiven anyway, why worry? Now, there is a strange idea of love! Do you really think that God cannot see in our hearts and that we can so easily manipulate Him? Anyone who thinks this way has never really loved. Love has no ulterior motives. St. Paul, extolling the virtues of love, wrote: "Love bears everything, believes in everything, hopes for everything, endures everything" (1 Cor. 13:7), but he never said that love figures everything out in order to take advantage of everything! How could anyone think that the prodigal son, knowing his father's love and kindness, would try and squeeze more money out of him to go and squander it again? That would be a selfish, self-centered act, not the sign of an open heart to the Father.

Isn't it the same when it comes to Alcoholics Anonymous? An alcoholic, who for years has been unable to abstain from alcohol, will nonetheless always be welcomed, understood—"forgiven" so to speak—and allowed to participate freely in the group's activities. Under these circumstances, some might object—no punishment, no dismissal—why bother staying sober! And yet, this freedom, this "guarantee" of forgiveness, remains one of Alcoholics Anonymous' great strengths. Love, after all, is also freedom. In spite of the fact that A.A. members are free to drink, more than a million of them have not drunk a single glass of alcohol in the sixty years of the movement's existence (1935-1995).

A.A. doesn't only trust the alcoholics themselves, but relies especially on God's help. A true alcoholic, on his own, will go back to drinking. He goes back to drinking because he is "closed in" on himself, and his situation is likely to worsen each time. Let him open his heart to the Love of God, and he will be received at the banquet of sobriety and serenity.

Please believe me: anyone who opens his heart to God's Love cannot go back to his old habits. He is changed. It is God who has brought about this change, this transformation, this transfiguration. But if I can transform myself, you say, why do I need God? A change for the better can only come from one better than me, not from my equal.

On the other hand, just because we have put ourselves in God's hands and opened our heart to His Love, it would be absurd to think that we won't ever need to be forgiven again. Let's not conclude too hastily that the prodigal son is through with his wild ways, or that his father's troubles are over. If you have children, you know what I mean. The prodigal son is still young; let's imagine the rest of his life. He will follow the normal course for all human beings: he will probably marry, have children, grand-children, relatives, friends, servants and neighbours. However, the fact that twenty-five years earlier he had come home repentant to throw himself in his father's arms does not mean that he is expected never to do anything foolish again, that future forgiveness would be denied. I would like to think that from living with the Father, watching Him and listening to Him, we must become more like Him every day. How could we be in close contact with God and not become meeker, more trusting, more open to others, happier! If this transformation is not instantaneous, it is no doubt because the Father, out of Love, shows consideration for our fears, our hesitations and our limits. If we threw ourselves whole-heartedly into His arms, we would be immediately transformed. But instead, we do it very cautiously, holding back a little, for fear He will snatch us away too quickly from worldly goods, from our illusions of happiness, from our old loves. It will take God just as long to transform us as it takes us to completely give in to His love. It is difficult for God to be able to talk to us, to reach us, to teach, to educate, to mould us; we are never home! We are always looking for happiness elsewhere. As we get bored staying "at home", we go "downtown", seeking out purveyors of illusions. We stay home only on stormy nights, when we are deeply unhappy or afraid. These are the only times the Father can comfort us and teach us love. The day will doubtless come when nothing will feel better than staying home with our Father, learning to be His sons.

We have come to the end of our "Search for a Superior Being." May you have recognized in the God of our childhood all the love you have ever dreamt of, all the warmth and understanding you have ever needed.

Since we have discovered Love, it is now time to take the road back home. Sons and daughters, come along! Pick up your travelling gear and walk two by two. Let's hurry now, the Father is waiting! He has a party all ready for us; let's run there with joyful hearts: our turn has come to hear words of love!

The Dwelling Place of God

The Parable of the prodigal son returning home is primarily intended to make us understand the goodness and affection of the Father for the children that we are. Of course God does not live in a house located in any given area. However, the question remains: God being a pure Spirit, how can we find Him here on earth, every day, every minute of our lives? How can we serve God if we have no means of reaching Him? God is everywhere of course, but how can we meet Him tangibly, concretely?

God's favourite dwelling place is man. When He chose to reveal Himself to us, God became Man so that we could understand His message and see Him behind a human face. His Face continues to live behind mine, yours, behind all our faces: "Behold, I stand at the door and knock; if anyone hears my voice and opens the door, I will come in..." (Ap. 3:20). Once more, the symbol of a house is used, but this time, it's ours, our own inner home. God wishes, counts on, hopes to move into each one of us. We are "God's dwelling place", on the condition that we open the door for Him.

When we have opened the door of our hearts to Him, God comes in to stay. He settles down, becomes our constant companion and faithful friend, our guide and a very close sponsor. God lives within us. We are filled with His presence and no longer alone.

This awareness of God's presence within us gives unity to our whole being. If God were somewhere "out in space", in some far off country, we would have a tendency to "send" Him our life and our problems. However, it is "here and now" that we must live and face our difficulties, not "out there". God offers to be with us, every moment of our lives, and His presence makes itself felt in the courage to live rather than in magical solutions to life's problems. Jesus Himself tells us: "In the world, suffering awaits you. But take heart! I have overcome the world." (Jn 16:33)

If God lives within us, if He fills our emptiness, He now has the colour of our eyes and the size of our feet. Does that sound a little crazy? Without a doubt! However, the fact remains that God has no mouth to speak with, no hands to express Himself, no feet to take Him among men other than our own! How can God reach alcoholics in their misery except through us? And Al-Anons, Alateens, the lonely, the desperate? For "God's dwelling place" is also the "other" in front of me. God needs men and women like us to let everyone know that we are in God's embrace, that a great celebration is being prepared and that we are all invited.

We can only serve God by serving others. This does not imply that the other before me is God, but that the services rendered onto him, out of love for God, will be considered by God as personal favours: "Come, ye blessed of my Father... for I was hungry and you gave me food." Then the righteous will answer Him: "Lord, when did we see you hungry and feed you?" "Truly, I say to you, as you did it to one of the least of my brethren, you did it to me." (Mt. 25:31-40) These words of Love, in which God shows how much He loves the poor, the hungry, the desperate, to the point of considering the slightest gesture of compassion towards them as a personal favour, these very words are those of the Last Judgment that fill with fear so many Christians. God is behind evey face we meet. To greet a face is to greet God; to shut someone out is to shut God out.

"Come, ye blessed of my Father, for I knocked on the door of Alcoholics Anonymous and you welcomed me; I went to Al-Anon and you opened the door." "But, you will say with surprise, you never came to A.A., nor to Al-Anon! We never heard of you." "I certainly did, Jesus will answer; each time you received a newcomer, listened to him, encouraged him, understood him, consoled him, it was me you welcomed." "Then that old geezer who gave us so much trouble... it was you?" "Yes, it was I. And for all you have done, come, ye blessed of my Father..."

Part three

ENTRUSTING OURSELVES
TO SOMEONE ELSE'S CARE

Made a decision to turn our will and our lives over to the care of a God, as we understood Him."
Big Book

We have reached the third step of Alcoholic Anonymous, certainly the richest in our spiritual journey. Yet, it is just a beginning: learning to trust when we don't understand, when we can't explain the trials, the mystery of suffering and evil in the world, the meaning of life, sickness and death. Why do I exist? What am I here to accomplish? What is my mission? How can I best achieve it, and at the same time fully realize my potential? The answers are far from obvious. However, it is important that each individual define himself in relation to a mission which is uniquely his own. God alone can give meaning, direction, and inspiration to our lives; our own light is too faint to guide us. God must reveal us to ourselves—"who" we are, and "why" we exist. The Catechism of our childhood was right in saying that we were created to love God, to adore Him and to serve Him. Therein lies an eternal truth. Isn't everything else passing, ephemeral, finite? We cannot, however, avoid living also for these values, passing, ephemeral, finite as they are; isn't that what we ourselves are? Our misfortunes and misery arise from the fact that we give these values too great a place in our lives. For instance, as we mentioned before, human love is a worthy and beautiful value, but of itself insufficient, for it can never totally fulfill us. What spouse, what child, what mother, what friend will follow us to the grave? Nor can their arms hold us back from the brink; if we don't throw ourselves in the arms of the Father, where shall we turn? Our vocation is to be reunited with the Father. How can we achieve this? What path must we follow? What truths are the right ones for each one of us, what life choices the most suitable? Only Christ can show us the way: "I am the Way, the Life and the Truth" (Jn 14:6), which means your way, your life and your truth. I am convinced that true self-knowledge, the discovery of that which is best in us, can only come from God.

We all know the story of Mary-Magdalene who, universally scorned by the community, had become very close to those who followed Jesus. She couldn't possibly have foreseen this. Jesus revealed her true nature to her, showed her that she was generous and authentic. Tired of being rejected, humiliated, pointed out, she threw herself, weeping, at His feet. She had reached rock bottom and Jesus was her sole refuge. And He made a saint out of her! I am your way, your truth, and your life. Knowledge of God leads inevitably to knowledge of self.

Then there was a notorious rich man called Zaccheus, hated by all because he was stingy and hard on the poor. One day, Christ expressed the wish to stay at his place, which, of course, Zaccheus accepted. The crowd grumbled: "Think of it, he has chosen to stay at a sinner's house!" It was on this occasion that Christ revealed to the usurer his real self: he was much more generous and kind-hearted than he had ever thought. Zaccheus gave half his fortune to the poor; furthermore, he promised to repay four times over for any wrong he might have done. No one, not Zaccheus himself, neither his mother nor his friends, could have foreseen in him such capacity for giving. Only Jesus could reveal it to Zaccheus, and show him that he was no worse than anybody else and that he was as worthy of being loved. Mary Magdalene, Zaccheus and many more had within themselves a potential for generosity, kindness, openness to others which lack of understanding and hard-heartness had stifled. By accepting Christ, they chose another way, the path to self-discovery which leads to life.

The third step calls for a decision: to give one's entire trust, to believe without reservations that, once we have met Christ and accepted Him, the best in us has already begun to grow. God always brings out the very best in us. Did not Jesus live the very best in man? When we sincerely open ourselves to God, what follows? We embrace Love with all its colours: acceptance, kindness, understanding, gentleness, generosity, gratuitousness, patience, fidelity, forgiveness, courage... All that is left to do is to imitate the Model. Ask yourself: "What would Christ do in my place?" No need to hesitate about the answer, is there? And so it often—not always—happens that, out of Love for Christ, we do things we might not have done otherwise. And over the years, the colours of love deepen! But perfection, even in the best of us, will never be achieved. There will always be that long stretch of road that we won't be able to cover. Through His suffering, His death and His resurrection, Jesus walked it for us. That is Redemption.

To entrust our life to Him means living according to the plan that God's Love conceived for us from all eternity. To put our will in God's hands means leaving it up to God to decide, and finally consenting to happiness on His terms. It also means learning how to simplify happiness, becoming detached. It takes a long time. I believe that God wants us to live standing up courageously, as men and women, not door mats. As to what God is asking of us in the short run, nothing less than prayer will help, and there will be long periods of waiting before we see the light. That's what Alcoholics Anonymous thinks at any rate, when it states in Step eleven that, through prayer and meditation, we shall come to know God's will for us, and at the same time, be given the courage to live.

Part four

DRAWING FROM THE SOURCE

*Sought through prayer and meditation to improve our conscious contact with God **as we understood Him**, praying only for knowledge of His Will for us and the power to carry that out.*
Big Book

We have now come to prayer and meditation. The eleventh step of Alcoholics Anonymous is a continuation of the third step and furthers the daily practice of the latter. As a matter of fact, the first nine steps are steps in the discovery of self, which lead to decisions on our part, and take us on into reflection and personal commitments. The three last steps, 10, 11 and 12, require life-long practice. Thus, the eleventh step naturally develops the third step. It stands to reason that no one will wait to have completed steps four to ten before praying; that might take years. It is normal that, having encountered God, we immediately begin talking with Him, sharing our secrets, our joys, our sorrows, in short, praying in order to deepen the first contact, strengthen that original commitment of step three.

One doesn't have to be kneeling in order to pray. Praying is first and foremost being conscious of a

Presence: it is to believe that there is someone there, to know in one's heart that one is no longer alone. One's whole field of consciousness is overcome by the idea that Someone has entered in the very "core of our being", that God dwells within. Praying is to feel, without any words being spoken, that we are in the house of the Father, that He is there, very close, wherever we may be: at home, at work, behind the steering wheel of a car, in the street, everywhere. I like to refer to this conviction as "my magnificent obsession." However, there is nothing compulsive or obsessive about it. It is liberating and light, and yet, one is constantly thinking about it!

Praying also means setting aside some quality time to spend in this Presence, to talk and listen. Prayer is much more than "asking." Why not just talk with God, chat with Him: tell Him little things, complain, express joy, sorrow or anguish, as well as dissatisfaction? Do you remember how some nuns and brothers, years ago, used to show their dissatisfaction by turning the statues' faces to the wall? Praying means unburdening one's heart with God as one would with a sponsor or a very close friend. You don't have to worry about hurting God's feelings, or tiring Him with your recriminations, your complaints, your moaning; isn't He our best Friend, the most patient, the most understanding, the most compassionate?

When those I sponsor have covered enough ground, I sometimes tell them: "Look, why not tell God everything you just told me?" But one must be willing to spend some time in prayer. Not surprising that we never know what God expects of us: we pray so little! A friend of mine, Mariette, sister of the Holy Cross, suggested that a good way to acquire the habit of prayer is to set aside a particular time for it, always the same, a time of day conducive to silence and meditation. She also said that, at first, a few minutes would be enough. It is quite possible that we may find prayer boring; we are used to conversing with real people, before us in the flesh. Prayer being an activity of the heart and the spirit, it will take some time to begin really enjoying it. Whatever the case may be, we must pray; it is absolutely essential. And let us not make the mistake of thinking "that God is at the other end of a line." If we find it enjoyable to share our difficulties and our joys with friends, it is far more important to share them with God.

Prayer is not a monologue in the presence of a silent, passive or absent God. We are in the habit of talking "non-stop", explaining to God at great length what He should do to direct our lives, and how He should go about it. As Louis Evely said, we always ask that our will be done, rarely God's! Most of our prayers aim at having God remove all the difficulties which are inherent to human life. After having explained to God what He must do, we feel we have done our share and can now rest. What part did God play in the conversation? None!

It is good that we tell God what is troubling us, but it's not up to us to tell Him what to do about it. Let us share what is close to our heart, what makes us sad or frightens us, and then, let us be silent and listen to what God has to say. We won't hear a voice or actual words. We would be frightened to death if we did! Just imagine hearing a voice in the night answering your prayers in very clear, precise words; you would be so afraid that you would call someone to reassure you. No. God answers our prayers by bringing about changes of mood: from fear, we move to a calm feeling of trust; from refusal to acceptance, from resentment to reconciliation, from inertia to action. During prayer, God can soothe us and bring us to accept in advance whatever may happen, whether or not it be according to our wishes. And that's a real miracle! The time we spend in silence listening to God makes our prayers fruitful. Listening to God doesn't mean that we expect an answer, but rather a change of heart. Listening to what God wants us to learn means trusting Him to guide us as He sees best, even when we are "in the dark". What kind of faith would we have if we could trust only after having been given assurances that everything would unfold according to our wishes? We can be sure of one thing only: God in His own good time—it may take years—is slowly but surely preparing happiness for us His way! How is He going to do it? I don't know. Are we going to be rich or poor, sick or healthy, alone or madly in love? I don't know. I only know that God can make us happy, in whatever way He chooses. Nothing else matters.

Praying also means checking to see if we are in God's range, in His colours. Why are we afraid? Because, not sporting His colours, we have slipped out of His range. God is Love, and Love brings security. "Why are you fearful, men of little faith?" Because we lack trust in God. Resentment is certainly not one of God's colours; if it flares up in us, we shall have to come back into God's range. God is forgiveness. With Him we are prepared to forgive, and in so doing, we recover joy and peace. Do we feel angry? Let us focus on God's colours. God is meekness; with Him, we shall be gentle and our anger will vanish. By dint of drinking at the Source of Divine Love, through prayer, we shall eventually, after years of trying, be a little more like Love itself. Love will transform us in His own image and likeness. Amen!

To pray is to listen anew to the Word of God after two thousand years. Having lived among us, He answered all our questions, because those living near Him in His time asked Him the same ones. The answers given by Jesus are for all times. Imagine an alcoholic asking Bill for advice; he would merely reiterate what he already said: admit your condition, believe, entrust your life... Hear the message once more. Those whose God lives somewhere out there, never to be seen or heard, will have difficulty getting Him to say anything. Luckily for us, we believe in a God who lived among us, who spoke to us. Nothing is more enriching—for Christians—than to meditate on a word, a parable, or an event in the life of the Lord. To meditate is to deeply reflect on the significance of the Word of God for each one of us, in our particular situation, at a given time. "Go, get rid of all your possessions, give the money to the poor, and follow me", Jesus told the wealthy young man. Now, how do these words apply to us today? We must first reflect on them. Is Jesus inviting us to sell all our belongings on the spot and give them to the poor? Not until we have found a valid reason for so doing. We can most certainly give a sum of money to the poor. But it would be ill-considered for us to sell our furniture, our car, and all we own, only to find ourselves wandering aimlessly on the street, eventually having to buy back everything we sold, since we all need a bed to sleep in and a chair to sit on! If someone feels called upon to give his life to a special cause, let him first seek a place with Jean Vanier or Mother Teresa, or in some other community. Then, he can sell his belongings, for he will have a reason to do so, a cause to "follow". Christ didn't invite the young man to part with all his riches, give the money to the poor, and then just stand there, doing nothing! This invitation to complete detachment was a prelude to a calling, and in the case of the wealthy young man, it certainly is among the most exacting in the Gospel. Others are much easier to obey, and present less of a risk.

"I have come that your joy may be complete." This statement by Jesus brings us to reflect on the reasons for which our joy is never, or rarely, perfect. Could it be that we hardly ever seek our joy in God, and that most of the time we seek it elsewhere? Similarly, we can reflect on God's compassionate love towards the prodigal son and Mary Magdalene; on the warnings concerning the pursuit of wealth, honours and prestige: "For where lies your treasure, there also is your heart." Words like: "I give you my peace, I leave you my peace" are fraught with love and consolation. We could go on and on, but this is enough to help us understand what it means to listen anew to God's message, two thousand years after it was given: words of love, acceptance, understanding and forgiveness.

The harsh words in the Gospel are not for you. Jesus uttered them for those who hardened their hearts against Him "refusing to see, refusing to hear," refusing to open their hearts to the Love of God and to the love of their neighbour. They were aimed at the proud, the Pharisees, at all those who stubbornly persisted in their rejection. The rest of you, go in peace, and sleep soundly; for I know, without having met you, how much your kind hearts are starved for love. Are you not also among "God's poor"?

Among the different types of prayers, let us consider those of petition, of thanksgiving, and of contemplation.

What should we ask God? That depends on whether we know what makes us happy. Do any of us really know? As far as I am concerned, I have been wrong so many times on the subject of my own happiness that I prefer to leave it up to God to decide for me. Come to think of it, if one expects EVERYTHING from God, there isn't anything left to ask Him. Only the courage and the strength to live according to His Will for us. Jesus taught that the Father knows our true needs better than we do. What then? Personally, I merely ask that the very best in me may grow, and for the insight I need to discover, through others, through daily events and the passing of time, what I must do and where I should go. That is all. The rest is of little consequence. "Therefore do not worry and ask: 'What shall we eat?' or 'What shall we wear?' Those are heathen concerns. Your heavenly Father knows all your needs. Seek first His Kingdom and His Justice, and all the rest shall be given to you. Therefore, do not be anxious about tomorrow; for tomorrow will take care of itself." (Mt 6:31-34)

The prayer of thanksgiving, an invigorating tonic against self-pity, fear and boredom, is a way of reflecting on all the favours that God has granted us since our last encounter. We thank Him for all His gifts: we are no longer thirsty, we have lacked neither shelter nor food; we have been blessed with new friends! What on earth could we complain about? Haven't we at least received the necessities of life? Didn't God take care of us to this day? Why would He suddenly stop? In the light of the past, we take heart for the future.

In the prayer of contemplation, we stand in silence before God. A moment of wonder in which we let God's love for us, just as we are, envelop us, basking in His light and His joy. Nothing can be as bracing, as restful, as refreshing.

These are but a few thoughts on prayer, and by no means an exhaustive study. If you so wish, you can find many books on the subject. Besides, you must know some persons already acquainted with prayer who would be delighted to share their experience with you and give you precious advice. Some have enjoyed being part of a prayer group. A wide variety of choices is at your disposal. However, let us remember that prayer is an important step in our spiritual journey: it is through prayer that we discover the Heart of God and draw closer to Him day by day. I don't believe I am mistaken when I say that, in general, we do not pray enough. Jesus stressed the importance of prayer; let us ask Him to give us a taste for it; in time, it will come. Just start with the word "Father"...

Part five

AN INWARD LOOK:
TAKING STOCK OF OUR LIVES

Made a searching and
fearless moral inventory of ourselves.
Big Book

Here we are: the chapter on the question of personal moral assessment may have caught your attention when you were looking through the table of contents. It may also have been recommended to you by someone who lent you this book, and suggested it as a helpful guide in making that assessment. However, I must urge you to read the preceding chapters first, in order to create within you the appropriate mood of love and openness without which the fourth step runs the risk of becoming nothing more than a cold, cerebral exercise. The personal inventory is the fourth of the twelve steps, and taking the time to think about the first three might be a good idea at this point. However, I do not rule out the possibility that you might be—much more than I was— spiritually ready to proceed and, in that case, I invite you to do so.

Although the *Big Book* of Alcoholics Anonymous provides an explanation of this inventory, the actual presentation of the exercise is difficult to grasp and poses a real problem for most people (a member, who is working on his Doctorate in psychology, recently phoned to tell me how utterly confused he was by the presentation of this step). With the exception of an example of how to draw up the "list of resentments", the whole chapter's casual style and lack of formal methodology allows each individual the freedom to proceed in his own way.

This part of my book is an attempt to explain the fourth step. We shall see what it is, and what it isn't, as well as the reasons for taking it. I also intend, starting with the *Big Book* of A.A., to present a precise model that anyone wishing to make a complete moral inventory can follow point by point.

The members of A.A., Al-Anons, Alateens, O.A. (*Overeaters Anonymous*) and G.A. (*Gamblers Anonymous*) are generally very much aware of the importance of this fourth step. Even those who have not yet taken the step have heard about it, and most of them have the intention of doing it. But I should like to add a word for those who do not belong to the aforementioned groups.

With the exception of the members of religious communities—and, of course, of those belonging to groups where the twelve steps are practised—it's quite rare to find someone engaged in a spiritual quest picking up a pencil and actually taking stock of his life in writing. Practising Catholics no doubt examine their conscience before going to confession, but what we are talking about here is a much more elaborate, complete and methodical self-assessment. Whoever wishes to evolve psychologically and spiritually should be able to fulfill the requirements of steps four and five of Alcoholics Anonymous. Labourers, professionals, priests, nuns or monarchs can all benefit so greatly from this exercise that it's hard to imagine that anyone wouldn't want to do it. And if we can do it, why couldn't you? I therefore invite my readers who are not members—both men and women—to read this chapter very carefully, and to follow the instructions with pencil in hand.

What is it all about? Looking, searching, becoming aware, reflecting on ourselves, questioning ourselves, discovering that, in some cases, we would be happier if we changed our attitude; attempting to develop, allowing the very best in us to grow and not block the source of life by our resentment, our fears, our stubbornness, our arrogant certainties, our eternal regrets, our lack of trust, our exclusion of others, and so on.

It is not an analysis of our aptitudes, our tastes, or our potential, but a "moral" inventory. For example, courage, forbearance, mildness, the capacity to forgive, to accept all belong to the "moral" order. You have doubtlessly recognized God's colours... which we should all try to reflect in our lives. Hence, this type of assessment is an attempt "to examine those things in us which have prevented us from moving forward", or if you prefer, from living in God's range of colours.

It is extremely important to understand that the aim of the fourth step in A.A. is not knowledge of the whole self, but of one part of the self, one aspect of what we are. Also to be noted is that the goal of this type of moral inventory is not to list the qualities or "positive" aspects of a person. I do not minimize the importance of becoming aware of what is good, what is positive in us; in step four, we do exactly that by asking God to eradicate all that stifles our "better self", to separate the wheat from the chaff. But, at this stage, it is not so much our qualities that concern us, but rather our deficiencies or flaws of character. Since the self-assessment aims at examining our negative side, in no way can it lead— and this bears repeating—to knowledge of the self. Rather, it will shed light in the dark corners of our personality, the negative zones which we have been careful to avoid for fear of discovering that we are at fault. It is true that, in the past, we may have felt so lonely, and needed so much to be loved, to retain what little self-esteem we had, that, had we stumbled on our negative zones, we might never have had the strength to face them and survive. But now, we have discovered a God of Love who is always willing to help and encourage us; we are no longer alone. That is why it is preferable to make the moral inventory only after having found God, the only One capable of accepting us as we are, who never condemns but always forgives; who, instead of harping on our sinful past, takes our hand and faces the future with us, showing us the way to a better and happier life. Mary Madgalene, the good thief, the adulteress did not have to hand over a fifty-page inventory of their sins before being accepted. Long before we found God, and long before we made our self-assessment, each one of us already knew, deep down, his failings, his deficiencies, his weaknesses.

Was it not, in fact, precisely because of these failings and weaknesses that, for so long, we felt unworthy of our Father's love? Whoever, in step three, has entrusted himself to God knows that he has been accepted unconditionally. We do not make a moral inventory in order to be accepted, forgiven, loved more : God accepted us, forgave and loved us even before the creation of the world. Do you think that it is God who refuses to forgive, or we who do not believe in His forgiveness? That's the whole point. It's not unlikely that Mary

Magdalene, having become aware of many other short-comings — some more subtle, but no less real—talked them over with Jesus and His disciples, and in time, with God's grace, she was slowly transformed. Our moral inventory invites us, as it did Mary Magdalene, to go deeper, further, and to continue to grow with the help of God of whose love we are already sure.

Therefore, this step will not be undertaken to find out "who I am" but "where I stand." Forgive me for insisting on this point, but I would not want this assessment to become an exercise in self-flagellation. God is not asking us to humiliate ourselves, but to humble our-selves. It's hardly the same thing! Nothing is more painful than seeing a man who has been "humiliated", beaten and crushed. Our defeat to alcohol, our despon-dency, our self-destruction find meaning and value only when we "stand up again" in a recovery made possible by our Father's goodness. Alcohol has debased us, I will grant you that; but it's inconceivable that any of the A.A. steps should do the same. Does the fourth step teach humility? Yes, but very little. This step will reveal our pride to us but will barely make us more humble. God alone will achieve that by making us truer to ourselves. That will be in step seven: "Humbly asked Him to remove our shortcomings." This step will, in time, transform us. We will discuss it in another chapter. A moral inventory will make us "see" our deficiencies; it will not correct them.

Many expect too much, too soon from this self-assess-ment, followed in step five by their talking about it to someone else, after which they believe they are wholly transformed. A friend of mine, a member of A.A. with a sense of humour, was recently reminding of that: "Yes, my dear! Some years ago, after having completed step

four, and talked about, I thought I was completely changed; I really thought I was perfect!" This step is just one
of the milestones on the way to change; after steps five
and six, we are ready, in step seven, to ask God for the
transformation we wish. It seems as though the fourth
step is thought of as some kind of miracle, more
important than our encounter with God. When things are
not going well with someone, we are likely to tell them
that it's because they haven't understood step one, or
else step four. That may be true in some cases, but it's
definitely not the rule! Rarely do we tell them that the
real problem may lie in their relationship with God,
which may be superficial, in their wavering trust in Him,
or their unwillingness to put themselves in His hands.

Why a moral assessment? Why is it so important that
I acknowledge my deficiencies? Because if I don't
acknowledge, for example, that I am inclined to anger, I
will not be able to ask God to free me from it! If Leona
"doesn't see", "won't admit" that she is a liar, because
she has never taken the trouble to examine her behaviour, how is she going to ask God to make her truthful?
She doesn't "see" herself as a liar. This fourth step is to
our deficiencies what the first step is to alcohol. Someone who "doesn't see", "doesn't admit" that he has an
alcohol problem will certainly not be inclined to ask
God's help in solving a problem he doesn't have! And
so it is with our faults. Some people are absolutely
unaware that they have character flaws that make them
unbearable. For example, Mrs. Critical never has a kind
word for anybody, complains incessantly about her
husband, her daughter, her son, her neighbours, the
times we are living in, the weather... You know the
type! Tell her that she is negative and she will answer
that you do nothing but criticize her, as you do every-

body else. She can't "see herself". Somebody else tends to exaggerate, to distort reality, and you draw his attention to the fact. Answer: "That's it! Call me a liar while you are at it!" Never having put down on paper what "he sees" in himself, he doesn't know himself. To see, one must look. "Did you see that bear lumbering towards the river? No, I wasn't looking!"

This written assessment will help you to remember when, in step five, you meet with a person of your choice to reveal its contents: "Admitted to God, to ourselves, and to another human being the exact nature of our wrongs." In order to admit them, we must necessarily have taken a good look at them. Finally,— as I have already said— he moral assessment will allow us to perceive clearly what we are going to ask God to eliminate in us.

Once we have completed step four, we realize it wasn't half as bad as we thought. However, for a person who is about to embark on it, the prospect is anything but exciting. Quite the contrary. To undertake such a disheartening task, we'll need courage: "Made a searching and *fearless*..." God will give it to us, and knowing that He will be at our side, we can be sure of success. The sponsors also play a role in this step by supporting and encouraging the newcomers.

A last word of advice before we begin: don't make the mistake of thinking that one or two hours of work will suffice. Much, much more time will be required. In the method suggested, the written assessment is divided into well-defined parts; one can thus proceed point by point, at a rate of no more than half an hour or an hour at a time, and come back to it the next day or several days later. There is no reason why one can't take, say, a month to complete the assessment. No need to rush.

Some prefer to retire to a quiet spot and spend two, three or even four whole days on it. It's just a question of personal preference. With people who can't write, someone should follow the method suggested point by point and ask them pertinent questions. In all other cases, this procedure must be avoided. Writing down things oneself, as we shall see, has definite advantages.

Generally speaking and without much discussion, members are increasingly willing to make their assessment in "writing". But there are still a few who don't understand the necessity of "writing" down something which is perfectly clear in "their head". This way of thinking is probably due to the fact that, in the past, members had the impression they were practising the fourth step "when they told the story of their life". The idea is not to tell the story of your life as you would in a novel; that much is perfectly clear when we follow the procedure outlined in the book *Alcoholics Anonymous*. For those who are not convinced of the importance of making a "written" assessment, here are a few references:

The A.A. book in eleven instances asks that we "write" down what we have discovered. Moreover, the model list of resentments, in three columns, brings the number to twelve. Here they are:

1. "When we are working on our resentments, *we write them down on paper*." Page 64, *Big Book*.

2. "*To our list* of resentments, we add..." Page 65

3. "Generally, we indicate as many specific points as does the following example:" (This example is the *list* of resentments drawn up in three columns.) Page 65

4. "We return to our *list*..." Page 66

5. "We go over our *list*..." Page 67

6. "When we discovered our faults, we *listed* them." Page 67

7. "We have put them *in black and white* before us." Page 67

8. "We have *written them (our fears) on paper*..." Page 66

9. "We have *written everything down on paper, and have studied this document*." Page 70

10. "... we have *written* many things." Page 70

11. "We have *made a list* of our resentments and we have analyzed them." Page 70

12. "We have *made a list* of the persons..." Page 70

This, I believe, should dispel any lingering doubts!

The advantages of writing are unquestionable; one's thoughts are consigned to paper in an orderly fashion, so that there is no need to go over them once again. As we well know, memory is a faculty that forgets! Shoppers save time and energy by drawing up a list of what they have to buy. The successful business man keeps a daily agenda. Why would a moral inventory not benefit from this sensible and practical approach?

The Method:
Practical Organization of the Moral Inventory

It's time to get ready: you will need a ball-point and some paper. It is preferable to use standard size paper

(8 1/2" x 11".) rather than a stenographer's pad which does not afford sufficient space.

Have your copy of the *Big Book* close at hand. You should read carefully the section dealing with the fourth step; it will enable you to judge how closely the method presented below conforms to the norms of A.A.

Those who do not have the *Big Book* of A.A. will have to make do with the instructions given here. I have followed, as closely as possible, the letter of the *Big Book*, but better yet, its "spirit". Here are, as a reference, the key phrases from the *Big Book* which serve to justify the model that follows:

1. "When we tackle our resentments, we first make a list of them on paper." Page 64

2. "...we have realized that the people who have wronged us were perhaps spiritually ill." Pages 66-67

3. "Refusing to dwell on the wrongs of others towards us, we courageously examine our own faults." Page 67

4. "We have carefully gone over all our fears." Page 68

5. "We all have sexual problems. We would scarcely be human if we had none." Page 69

6. "...and if you have made a list of your main faults..." Page 72 (the universal list includes: pride, anger, envy, jealousy, slander, calumny, etc.)

7. "...and then we felt sorry for ourselves". Page 86

First Point of the Moral Inventory:
Draw up a List of Resentments

Let us consider the word itself: resentment. A strong, deeply felt resentment will be accompanied by anger and sometimes even by a desire for revenge. However, a slight resentment might simply mean that we are experiencing a "feeling again" ("re-sent": to feel anew). For instance, let's suppose someone has caused us pain; every time the name of that person is mentioned, or we happen to think of him, or meet him/her, we "re-sent", or feel anew the hurt, the injustice or the insult, without necessarily hating that person to the point of wishing for revenge. A resentment is sometimes expressed in these terms: I don't wish this person any harm, but I would rather not meet him/her, nor hear about that person. This attitude doesn't pose any problem with strangers, but it may be uncomfortable and embarrassing if a close relative is involved. Whatever the case may be, the point of the exercise for now is not to know whether we should change our attitude toward one particular person, but rather to list the persons we resent.

The importance of getting rid of our resentments can never be stressed enough. They are the opposite of love and, as such, they keep us dangerously far from God's range and the evangelical Message, closing our hearts to the very source of life. "Resentment is the main enemy. It destroys more alcoholics than anything else." Clearly, a life full of resentment can only lead to futility and unhappiness. Inasmuch as we allow resentment to control us, we waste precious hours of our lives. For an alcoholic, whose hope lies in maintaining and improving a spiritual experience, harbouring grudges is a very serious problem. We have learned that it could even be fatal, since it prevents the Holy Spirit from reaching us.

Before starting the list of resentments, it would be well to divide the sheet into three columns using vertical lines from top to bottom.

In the column on the left, write the **names** of the persons you resent. In the center column, write the nature of the **offence** that caused—and is still causing—the resentment. In the **column on the right**, by far the most important of the three, list what was most deeply hurt in you: your **pride**, your sense of **security**, your **ambitions**, your **personal relationships** (including sex). "In most cases, we shall discover that our self-esteem, our pocketbook, our ambitions, our personal relationships (including sex) have been hurt or threatened. That is why we were bitter, boiling inside." (pp. 64-65, *Big Book*)

Sometimes resentment may well date back to early childhood. A teacher may have hurt your feelings and you have bad memories of him. Furthermore, if that teacher was a nun or a priest, you may well feel bitter towards the entire clergy and anything that has to do with religion. Hence the necessity to list resentments all the way from childhood to the present.

It is important here to note that there is no need to rack one's brains to find as many names as possible. If a resentment does exist, it will flare up very quickly! Some people are less inclined than others to resentment; if you are one of them, you will have few names to write down. However, most people will feel at some point in their life some bitterness or irritation against someone, and the resentment usually lasts. Think about it! We don't mean "hate", but "feeling that way again."

It is now time to make the list, which we will divide into six parts:

1. Chilhood.

2. Adolescence.

3. Adulthood (the period in our life since we have become independent... since we have begun to live alone.

4. Married life.

5. At work.

6. With A.A. or similar associations.

1. Childhood (at home: our parents, brothers and sisters, uncles and aunts, servants... at school: teachers, classmates...)

I am resentful of	Cause	How I was hurt
1. Sister Saint X	Teacher in a particular convent school, humiliated me before the class. I was afraid they would take me for an idiot... they laughed at me...	My ego was wounded (**pride**). **Fear** of being laughed at (**personal prestige**).

| 2. Aunt Rose | Grumpy and sour tempered, exaggerated my faults and was responsible for having me punished unjustly... | Wounded ego (**pride**) and fear of being punished because of her (**fear and insecurity**). |

If you look at the column on the right, you will see that **fear**, **insecurity** as well as **pride** and **self-esteem** are always involved. Note that in the case of Aunt Rose, we are justified in holding it against her for having been unfair towards us; the point is that we are resentful and so we must write it down. (The injustice is Aunt Rose's problem.) In the center column, the cause of the offence can be summed up in just a few words: you're not writing a novel. These notes will serve as reminders when the time comes to confide in another person (fifth step), at which point we can elaborate on what happened.

2. Adolescence (at home... at school... teachers... friends... family... relatives...)

I am resentful of	*Cause*	*How I was hurt*
3. Jeanne X	She was fifteen, and would never dance with me... even refused to talk to me... She preferred the tall, insignificant XY.	Felt rejected, hurt in my **pride**.

| 4. A student | Tall and hand-some. First in the class, admired by the teachers... I was jealous. | **(Jealousy), fear** of not being loved and admired **(personal prestige).** |

Case 4. Brings up **jealousy** in the third column. It should be replaced by **fear** and wounded **pride**, since **jealousy** is actually the **fear** of not looking as well as someone else, the **fear** of losing someone we love... which obviously hurts our sense of **self-esteem** (**pride**).

3. **Adulthood** (the period in our life since we have become independent, since we have begun to live alone)

I am resentful of	*Cause*	*How I was hurt*
5. Mrs. McNutt	She is "nuts", she looks down on me, talks against me to my friends, and was responsible for my quarrelling with one of them.	**Personal relationships**, my **pride** was hurt... **Fear** of her carrying on this way...

Once again: even if some people "deserve" to be blamed because they might have wronged us, we include their names without taking into account their degree of responsibility. What we are interested in are our personal reactions and our wounds, nothing else.

4. Married life (spouse, in-laws... friends... servants...)

I am resentful of:	Cause	How I was hurt
6. My wife	She is always criticizing me... she is probably having an affair with Smith... Wants the house in her name.	Hurt in my **pride**. **Personal and sexual relationships** threatened (**fear, insecurity**). **Finances** also threatened.
7. My father-in-law		

5. At work (boss, managers, co-workers, etc.)

I am resentful of:	Cause	How I was hurt
8. The boss		
9. The accountant		

6. A.A. or similar associations

I am resentful of:	Cause	How I was hurt
10. Roberta X	She wants to "run" the group. She even criticized my message...	**Fear** she might harm the group; my **pride** was hurt.
11. Eugene G.	Always talking about God.	Felt attacked in my beliefs and deep personal convictions (**pride**).

| 12. Leopold T. | Doesn't talk enough about God; talks of nothing but his drunken brawls; is very vulgar. | Felt attacked in my beliefs and deep personal convictions (**pride**) and **fear** for my spiritual values... |

At A.A., especially in the first years, we "fear" that our personal convictions will be contested. Any opinion differing from our own is perceived as a personal attack. However, with the years, this feeling tends to disappear as we become more emotionally stable. We have learned that the only A.A. that really matters is "one's own". We have noticed that each one of us expresses—as well as can be done—what is most deeply felt at any "given moment." The newcomers, on their arrival, should be made to understand the utmost importance of complete freedom of expression. Should that freedom be denied any member, your freedom of expression, by the same token, will be diminished to the same degree when your turn comes to speak. Besides, doesn't each person try to offer his best? Don't you? We all know too well the deep hurt caused by destructive criticism. The members of A.A. do not claim to be professionals, and they have the right to our respect and gratitude, not our judgment. If one of the members is not to our liking, we know from experience that it's best to simply forget about him. To talk about him incessantly will merely fuel our resentment, and will not change his way of seeing things. And, if we had the opportunity of getting to know him better, we just might change our mind about him. Very often, as we get to know people better, we learn to love them. No harm in trying!

Let us now list the institutions and principles that make us **feel resentful**:

I resent	Cause	How I was hurt
The government		
The clergy		
Doctors		
The police		
The rich		
Educated people		
Blacks, Jews, or other races		
The question of God		
Some women have something against other women		
Some women have something against men		
Some men have something against women		
etc.		

The **column on the right** being the most important, let us look at it first. We will notice that it's our "pride" that is hurt most often, if not always. Our **self-esteem** has certainly taken a knock! And our wounded "little ego" rebels, gets angry and rants on about those ill-mannered louts who dared attack it! What other reason would there be for us to get angry at anyone? Suppose that, in front of some friends of yours, someone criticized a certain building, calling it heavy, ugly, boring, you might readily agree, unless... you were the architect! When the **ego** feels attacked in the sensitive areas of one's profession, taste, artistic sense, it bristles with anger and resentment ensues.

If we could be less concerned about ourselves, everything would be so much easier, more peaceful and harmonious. Besides, our worth as a human being has very little to do with "what others think of us", but a lot with "what *we are*." If you are a good architect and aware of it, you can evaluate your own work without being the least bothered by someone's unpleasant remarks. Would you believe that you were a genius just because somebody thought so? So don't you go believing that your are worthless because somebody says it! Let us be "ourselves", and cut our **ego** down to size: that's true humility! Unfortunately, we tend more to act like the frog from the well-known fable: we blow up our **ego** out of proportion until it bursts! But just because I wrote these lines and you have read them doesn't mean that we will be able to see ourselves more realistically. But at least we realize it is necessary, and that's already something.

If we are convinced that God loves us as we are, we won't feel the need to inflate our **ego** as much. And if, in addition, we pay attention to the love of those around us, our **self** will be better off for it.

Second Point of the Moral Inventory

The paper need not be divided into three columns. The model given below is to be followed. It is important to go over all the names that appear on our list of resentments, and to take the time to think about each one. Let's say that the first person listed is your father; your reflection could go as follows:

My father. What kind of life did he have? Was he happy? Was he able to express himself? Did he not suffer himself a great deal? Had he been happy, fulfilled, liberated, would he have treated his children differently?

Having thus reflected, we begin to understand the suffering of others, to realize that, had they been happier, they would have been more open and understanding. At this point **we must consent—with God's grace—to forgive**. This last sentence calls for an explanation. We know that forgiveness is an expression of love, its very criterion. It is thus almost impossible to forgive someone we hate and, without God's help, it's not likely that we will be able to forgive from the bottom of our hearts. Indeed, if a parent can forgive a child out of love—although that may not be easy, at times—one can understand how difficult it is to forgive when there is no love. This prayer may help: "My God, I am incapable of forgiving, but 'I consent', I am willing to forgive, because of You, for You who are asking me to do so. Lead me, gradually, with time, to this forgiveness." Because we relate to God in Love, it will be relatively easier to forgive "because of our love for

God", who is asking us to do so, than for the love of a person "whom we do not love." It's enough for us to "consent **with** God" to forgive, and to renew this consent every time resentment wells up within us. You will feel God's love transforming your heart.

We move on to the second name on the list. It may be that of a nun or a priest who gave you a hard time some time in the past. We write the name down, and think about it.

Sister Saint X. How old could she have been? Was she qualified for the job she had been assigned? Was what she did really that bad? Did it leave me permanently scarred? Could it not be that, because of my tender age, I exaggerated the importance of what she said? Was she happy in her vocation, at a time when no nun would have dared leave the Church even if she regretted having taken the veil? Etc.

Once again, we must be careful not to identify all the nuns with Sister Saint X. Were there not some in the community who were kind to you, who gave you attention and comforted you? Whatever the case may be, it is now time, after twenty years or more, to put an end to old resentments. Let's "consent with God" to forgive. Be generous, in your heart, and it will come! If we want to be happy, we must agree to leave the zone of petty resentments and move, with absolute determination, into that of God, which is love and forgiveness.

We must consent in this way to forgive all those whose names appear on the list, remembering that only God can lead us to true forgiveness. Soon, wounds you thought would never heal will disappear, and in their place, peace and compassion will flourish. It's God's miracle, the miracle of Love. They say that love can't be bought. Well, let's say that you can buy love with forgiveness.

Before undertaking the third point of the written moral inventory, I would like to say something: if you are tired, stop. Don't overdo it; you can pick up where you left off later. It could very well be that you are wondering about the usefulness of bringing up old quarrels? Wouldn't it be better to forget, to chase away all these upsetting memories from our mind? Besides, doesn't A.A. strongly recommend to live twenty-four hours at a time without worrying about the past or the future? "Do not look back, people say; you risk being hurt for nothing; if something weighs on your mind, dismiss it." This type of mental defence sounds a lot like repression in the Freudian sense, "a mental process whereby thoughts which are unbearable to the conscious mind are relegated to the unconscious. Although repressed in the unconscious, these thoughts remain active. They influence the emotional life of the subject and the Ego must struggle to keep them from resurfacing to the conscious mind."

I am going to give you a trick for handling thoughts without having to repress them. Suppose that, when you were drinking heavily, you had made a spectacle of yourself at a ritzy affair. The memory of it comes back from time to time, and unable to bear it, you try to chase it away mentally. It will come back and you will have to fight it off again. What you must do is "accept" reality and let the humiliating scene "rise" to the conscious mind, and then, say to yourself: "It's useless for me to deny that, in the past, I made a monumental blunder." And, although it may hurt your pride, I recommend this prayer: "My God, you know how badly I feel when I think of it; but 'with You', I consent to face the fact that

I was foolish. I no longer want to avoid thinking about it. I accept—and please help me to accept—that I behaved like a complete idiot. Amen." I can assure you that if the same thought ever comes back, it will never hurt again. Why? Because your conscious mind has accepted the painful memory and, furthermore, you have sensed that God understood you and stood beside you in the difficult process of acceptance. Talk it over with your sponsor, or with a person you love and who loves you. Try! It is far better to accept the realities of the past than to run away from them.

Third Point of the Moral Inventory

We still need our list of resentments to proceed. We hold a grudge against certain persons for given reasons. However, could it be that we ourselves have wronged these same people? If such is the case, we will write their names on a separate sheet which must be kept for the eighth step. "Banishing from our minds the wrongs of others toward us, we have resolved to examine our own faults. When were we selfish, dishonest, self-centered and frightened?" (*Big Book*)

For example, we listed our sister-in-law on our list of resentments:

My sister-in-law. My sister-in-law has never missed an opportunity to call me a good-for-nothing drunk and a sponger. But, to be honest, I did borrow from her husband—my brother—4000$, and when she reminded me the sum was due, I called her a petty miser. I added that this matter was between my brother and me, and she could just "shut up". (Pride—Fear of having to repay the debt—Selfishness—Dishonesty—Insolence.) One can easily understand why the sister-in-law got aggressive.

We do the same for each of the other names on the list. If we discover that we have wronged eight people, say on a list of fifteen, we shall write eight names on the separate sheet mentioned above. As for paying the 4000$ debt, and making amends for any other wrongdoing, we shall discuss it in the ninth step. It's too soon to worry about that. We're neither ready nor strong enough yet. We still have four steps to go.

Fourth Point of the Moral Inventory

It's time to learn to forgive ourselves. Without falling into the habit of minimizing the offence or our responsibility in it, it's important to realize that getting all worked up about it, dramatizing and refusing to forgive ourselves won't help matters a bit. Such conduct would only question God's Forgiveness. And, as we have seen, forgiveness is the test of love. Since God is Love, God always forgives; only human beings rarely forgive from the bottom of their heart. God does not categorize us according to our past, but finds joy in taking our hand in His and contemplating with us what we hope to become. If God is willing to forgive so generously, why should we stand in the way of Life by refusing to forgive ourselves? "We" are always the ones who close the door to His love and forgiveness.

The fourth point therefore consists of "consenting, with God, to forgive ourselves." In some cases, to forgive oneself is extremely difficult, as in the following example. A mother, to refill her glass, leaves her baby sitting on a table; she has to answer the phone and forgets all about the child who falls, and as a result, remains crippled for life. Every time she sees her grownup daughter with one leg shorter than the other, this woman is reminded of what she did: "I have forgiven myself, she confided to me, but it took nothing less than God's help to succeed." In such distressing cases, this prayer might be good: "My God, I can't forget, I can't forgive myself, but because of You, who forgive me, I am willing to forgive myself. Grant me Your help, so that I may come to accept this sad reality in my life. Amen." This exercise in forgiveness must be repeated for each name—we had eight—and that will complete the fourth point of the moral inventory.

Fifth Point of the Moral Inventory

This point seriously examines our **fears**. We have already admitted (in the right column of our list of resentments) to several fears, such as not making a good impression, being loved or admired less, being hurt in our pocketbook, losing someone we love, and so on. All of us—alcoholics or not—are subject to fears: worries over the economic situation, illness, old age, solitude and death. Some fear for their children, others for their parents; others still for themselves. These fears may be justified, but sometimes, they are totally groundless. But in any case, fear is absolutely useless, and always a bad counsellor; one should never act under its influence. Better to pray first and calm down, and confide our fear to our sponsor. Only then can we hope to act with proper judgment.

That having been said, fear should not be confused with prudence, which is a virtue. It would be silly, under the pretext of conquering fear, to act rashly. Before making certain decisions, we must learn to wait, to consult and examine the "pros and cons." And be careful not to assume that A.A. members—including the sponsors—always have the competence required to handle any case. If, for instance, your problem is a legal one, consult a lawyer. He could very well belong to A.A., but you are consulting him as a lawyer, not as a member.

Therefore: "We have gone over all our fears. We have written them down on paper, even those not associated with resentment. We have asked ourselves why these fears filled us." (*Big Book*) No one can predict with certainty what his life will be in a few years, not even in the coming months. Besides, many problems that require immediate solutions will leave you disarmed and powerless. What can you do for your twenty-year old daughter or son, in whom you had placed all your hopes, and who now roams the streets in search of drugs and alcohol? Leave it up to God, believe, hope, wait and love.

For each of the fears we put down on paper, we ask ourselves if it is founded. If so, what can we do about it? If you can do something, go ahead and do it. Then, leave it up to God. However, it bears repeating that, if taking some kind of action is an option, we must first reflect, consult and then act calmly.

Before concluding the fifth point of our inventory, I should like to add that a certain degree of worry and anxiety is a normal part of life. It's hard to imagine a whole life completely free from worry or anxiety. Just because we belong to A.A. and live according to spiritual principles, it doesn' mean that we shall forever be immune from the worries that our father and mother, brothers and sisters, uncles and aunts have known, in spite of their strong religious beliefs. Life holds the same difficulties for believers and atheists alike! Faith should give us the "courage" to live in a climate of serenity in spite of everything, and help us to stand erect in the face of trouble without "dramatizing" the slightest anxiety. Finally, in moments of fear and anguish, it is essential that we pray. Christ Himself found no better solution. Answers come to those who wait in trust.

Not all forms of anxiety can be immediately overcome. We must, with God's help, be prepared to suffer. For example, in the case of a child who hovers between life and death. Our prayer could then be the following: "My God, with You, I accept this anguishing uncertainty, this terrible suffering, because long ago, You gave a meaning to anguish and suffering. Be with me during these painful moments, and give me the courage not to sink into despair. Amen." In truth, faith is not meant to remove our pain, but rather to give us the courage to bear it. Paul Claudel, the French writer, has this to say: "The Son of God did not come to destroy suffering, but to suffer with us. He did not come to destroy the cross but to be nailed to it."

List of my fears:

_____

_____

_____

_____

Sixth Point of the Moral Inventory

The topic here is sexual behavior. This area of human behavior is very complex: thousands of books have been written on the subject. Many sexologists, psychiatrists and psychoanalysts won't always be able to come up with the appropriate solutions. We shall certainly not presume to do better, and to offer a solution to all problems. All we wish to do is to invite the reader to stop and think about the question of sex, in the hope of shedding a little more light on it and preventing things from getting worse.

"We do not wish to arbitrate for any person in what pertains to sex. We all have sexual problems. We would hardly be human beings if we didn't. What can we do about it? We have reviewed our behavior during the past years. When were we **selfish**, **dishonest**, **thoughtless**? Whom did we harm? Did we, without cause, harbour feelings of **jealousy**, **suspicion**, or **bitterness**? When we were wrong, what should we have done instead of what we did? We have written it all down on paper and we have studied this document."

Sexual problems should be handled like any other problem. But did our education, in this area, prepare us to evaluate, in a calm and detached manner, our sexual behaviour? Hardly! I need not insist. But we must remember how Christ did not hesitate in accepting Mary Magdalene, how He forgave her and welcomed her in His group of friends, as He might have done with a thief, for instance. And didn't God Himself defiantly rise to the defence of the adulteress? However, one must be careful not to confuse "forgiveness" with "approval." God does not approve of our mistakes, even if He forgives them! He is calling us—and helping us with

His Grace—to have better judgment. Naturally, many of us will err again, and progress will be slow at times. Nevertheless, we should never be discouraged; we must trust that over the years, God will succeed where we always seem to fail. "We have asked God to show us the ideal, and to help us to live accordingly." (*Big Book*, p. 69)

We must now draw up our list for sexual behavior. Opposite each name, we shall ask ourselves the following questions:

When have we been:

   a) selfish?

   b) dishonest?

   c) thoughtless?

   d) whom did we harm?

Have we been, inexcusably, the cause of:

   a) jealousy?

   b) suspicion?

   c) bitterness, sorrow?

When we were wrong, how should we have behaved, rather than the way we did?

_____

_____

_____

Finally, "whatever ideal we choose, we must be prepared to grow in that direction. We must be willing to make amends for any harm we may have caused, ON CONDITION THAT WE NOT CAUSE AN EVEN GREATER HARM in so doing. In other words, we handle sex as we do any other problem. When we meditate, we ask God what we should do in a given situation. The right answer will come IF WE TRULY WISH IT." (*Big Book*, p. 69) (The capitals are mine.)

I should like to go back to that last sentence: "The right answer will come IF WE TRULY WISH IT." Some people have confided to me that it took them a long time before they really wanted to change in the area of sex. Many don't see the need to change. At any rate, one should not expect a sudden, definitive change when it comes to our deficiencies, as in the case of alcohol. Bill W. himself wrote "If faith and acceptance rid us of alcohol completely, they can only be relatively effective in solving our emotional problems. For example, he goes on, no one can be totally free from fear, anger and pride. We shall never attain perfect humility, or ideal love. Consequently, we can only expect a gradual improvement of most of our difficulties, with the occasional disappointing relapse. Our former attitude of 'all or nothing' must be dropped." It will take some individuals years to correct certain tendencies. And again, no one can ever boast of having attained perfection in any area. Others, who have been too deeply wounded, will never be able to recover their balance, and will have to accept to live with their psychological infirmities. Learning to live with one's unbalance is in itself a way of achieving a certain emotional balance.

"To sum up about sex, we honestly pray that we may find what our true ideal is, that we may obtain help, in doubtful situations, to exercise a sound judgment, and to have the strength needed to do good. If sex is causing us numerous problems, WE TRY TO HELP OTHERS MORE. We think of their needs and we try to help them find solutions. This happens to be the way to make us forget ourselves." (*Big Book*) (The capitals are mine.)

Seventh Point of the Moral Inventory

The seventh point is relatively easy: to list the objects of our self-pity. Although the *Big Book* of Alcoholics Anonymous does not analyze it systematically, it does mention self-pity. Some people spend most of their lives complaining about everything; they were "jinxed" from the start, "never had any luck," "never had a chance to get an education" and so on; you've heard it all before! These people tend to be negative and to indulge in self-pity. However, without being necessarily negative, don't we all, at one time or another, feel sorry for ourselves, for our fate, for life in general? It will help to list the objects of our self-pity so that we may ask God to give us the courage to accept the realities of life, and then to talk them over with someone. (Fifth step)

I have a tendency to feel sorry for myself, to complain and to whimper:

over the past:

If I had not been drinking... if my husband hadn't...
If that accident hadn't happened... (Everlasting regrets.)

over the present:

This house is not as nice as the one we had... My spouse doesn't understand me... Children today never

153

listen, what a world! If we had more money... Our friends... (Regret and fear.)

over the future:

If this goes on, what will become of us? If only I were younger... It's sad getting old... (Regret and fear.)

over myself:

I'm too tall, too small, too fat; if I were more beautiful... better educated... If I had travelled, grown up in a better environment... (Everlasting regrets). If I were not so shy... if I could express myself... (Lack of self-confidence, fear and regrets.)

over A.A. meetings:

I am not getting enough attention... (Insecurity.) I wasn't welcomed in that group... So and so said hurtful things to me...

As you can see, all these complaints express our refusal to accept the past and the present as fact. As for the future, whatever we may foresee is arbitrary, and things could turn out to be entirely different from what we imagined.

What shall we do? Our negative attitude won't become positive overnight; but we could, right away, try to develop a positive outlook by praying. Let us ask God to help us accept our past, as it was, once and for all, and to give us the courage to live the present; finally, let us trust Him with the future. Are we feeling sorry for ourselves? It's time to offer a prayer of gratitude, reflecting on all the blessings we have received, giving thanks for each one individually. Finally, "accepting" things as they are is a wonderful antidote against self-pity. This concludes the seventh point.

If you are tired, stop here; you can continue later. Don't try to complete your moral assessment in a state of fatigue: you wouldn't be as clear-minded. Have a coffee... relax.

Eighth Point of the Moral Inventory

"...And if you have taken stock of your main faults..." Cheer up; it's nearly finished. So far, we have found a great deal of pride and anxiety, fears, resentments and anger towards persons who have stepped on our toes. But, in relation to ourselves, what about pride, anger and violence, envy, avarice, laziness and gluttony? I haven't mentioned drunkenness because we are alcoholics and no longer drink, but all the "others" could include that in their list. As for lust, which wasn't mentioned specifically, it was dealt with in the sixth point on sexual behavior. We shall add the following:

a) selfishness, egocentrism, egotism;

b) lying, false witnessing, slander, calumny;

c) theft, fraud, other crimes;

d) persecution mania, segregation;

e) a critical attitude, criticism, intolerance;

f) purity of intention;

g) the money question—owning material goods;

h) the question of the "one great love";

i) anything else that might have been overlooked.

Pride

We have dealt with pride at great length in our list of resentments. We became aware that we were loathe to forgive any attack on our precious little Egos. Pride triggers a series of reactions of which resentment is the most immediate and very often the most violent. Resentment leads to anger, which in turn can breed a desire for revenge; revenge will take the form of calumny or slander, jealousy and envy, all giving rise to injustices of all sorts and leaving in their wake broken homes and estranged friends. Finally, pride is always accompanied by selfishness: indeed, a proud person, believing himself to be superior to others, finds it only natural to be solely entitled to everything. That is why, in the next few pages, we shall reflect on many human vices of which pride is, more often than not, the root. But it's no use upsetting ourselves over it: who is without pride? The only upsetting thing would be if we didn't recognize that fact. To be able to acknowledge our failings is a priceless asset; it awakens in us the desire to turn to God for help, and He will help if we let Him.

We shall now turn to milder forms of pride. One of them is **vanity**; vanity makes us act foolishly and extravagantly. We might, for instance, spend more than we can afford on furs, jewels, a car, etc. It will prompt a person to exaggerate what he does, what he owns, etc. It is a subtle form of pride.

If we recognize that we are vain, we write it down: I am vain. My vanity manifests itself in the following ways:

_____

_____

Another form of pride is **touchiness**: some people are overly sensitive and they are easily hurt. You can't say anything to them—they get peeved at the slightest remark, often very much to the point. They are always vexed, hurt, offended, outraged, taken aback, insulted, etc. Should you find this trait in you, don't be too upset; it's a sign that you need to be loved a lot, and that you overreact to the slightest failing in this department. If someone, for instance, didn't hold out his hand to you, you shouldn't assume that he was deliberately trying to hurt you; he probably just forgot. At any rate, the Love God has for you, and that which your friends at A.A. will show you will soon satisfy your infinite need for affection, and little by little, you will be less sensitive to the inevitable vexations of life.

Am I easily offended? If I am, was it deliberate on the part of those who supposedly have offended me?

_____

Is it that important? _____

What attitude should I adopt?

_____

To help you analyze your pride, here are a few handy excuses one often resorts to in such cases:

— Are not self-respect and legitimate pride virtues? (Of course! But is it worth getting all worked up about to the point of being unhappy?)

— Our honour is at stake.

— Our dignity.

— Our social position.

— "After all, I am the head of the family..."

— "I am better than he is."

— "I am more competent than he is, I have the degrees to prove it."

— "It was I, after all, who founded this group."

To conclude, let us ask ourselves what image we wanted to project—and still do—what we always dreamt of becoming.

Ever since I was a child, have I always longed for things life could never give me?

_____

Do I fear not being as smart as others?

_____

Do I think I am of superior intelligence? If I do, is it true in fact?

_____

Did I have hopes and dreams I did not achieve?

_____

Do I regret not being wealthier?

_____

More important?

_____

More admired? Adulated?

Can I accept myself as I am?

It seems that the difficulty is not so much in **accepting ourselves as we are**, but rather in **accepting not having become what we had dreamt of**. This kind of wounded pride often leads to self-depreciation, and blinds us to the beauty there is in us; it's a pity. To estimate our worth—in the right sense—let us count neither success nor failures; let us not display our diplomas, nor brag about our promotions; but let us count those who love us instead, those who have helped us and those we have tried to help. Therein lies our true worth and all our riches, the only way to become "somebody": be somebody for a few people. To hell with stardom!

Anger

Its side effects, so to speak, are **impatience**, **aggressiveness**, **bad moods**, **sulking** (an inner anger, somewhat like resentment). When do we get angry? Isn't it every time our pride is hurt, every time someone disagrees with us, since, naturally, we are always right? Whenever someone criticizes our past, our behaviour? Even if some of the reproaches laid against us are unjustified, may we not safely conclude that, more often than not, the root of our anger, violent or contained, lies in our wounded pride, and the fact that we think much too highly of ourselves?

With whom am I inclined to get angry? _____

Can I accept comments, reproaches? _____

When I am kept waiting, what is my reaction? _____

What kindles my anger? _____

Etc. _____

Violence

Unrestrained anger. It makes people lash out at those around them: they throw objects, become verbally or even physically abusive. Violence may lead to murder. If you can't explain your fits of anger, if you are overcome by rage to the point of not knowing who you are anymore, the following pages may help. First, a few questions which bear on violence when **not under the influence of alcohol.**

Am I violent (when not under the influence of alcohol)?

_____

When? Why?

_____

With whom?

_____

To the point of striking people?

_____

(Other considerations.)

Some people, who are generally described as quiet and peaceful, are subject to sudden, uncontrollable fits of anger, which push them to do things they sincerely regret. They confess being at a loss to explain what is happening to them. Indeed, they are lucid enough to see things for what they are, and realize that it isn't reasonable to have a fit because someone disagrees with them.

However, should you openly express an opinion different from theirs, and stick to it, you might well get punched in the nose. You'll get off with a shock!

If you can't explain your fits of anger, and acknowledge that this bothers you, allow me to tell you about **hypoglycaemia**. Bill W., founder of A.A. took a great interst in this question and even wrote a brochure on it. This brochure is not generally available to A.A. groups. It is specifically meant for doctors, and may be obtained on request. I am personally very interested in hypoglyceamia and have read several books on the subject. Being continually in contact with alcoholics, I myself underwent all the medical tests for hypoglycaemia with a view to documenting myself, and thus be better able to know what I was talking about.

Medical science teaches us—Bill also speaks of it— that 80% of alcoholics suffer from hypoglycaemia to varying degrees, some only very slightly. But let us see what this condition consists of.

I am not a doctor; however, what I am going to say on the subject is exact, if not exhaustive. Should you gather from this information that you are hypoglycaemic, you should consult your doctor. At any rate, the treatment, except in severe cases, is very simple.

Briefly, hypoglycaemia is an abnormally low blood sugar. Let us consider a mild case: the person feels somewhat tired; if he eats a chocolate bar, he immediately regains his vigor. The improvement is only apparent and temporary; the sugar level "rises" but "falls" rapidly, and the subject feels tired again. A vicious circle sets in. This case has been simplified to explain the "rise" and the "fall" of sugar in the blood. Many alcoholics feel tired at certain times of the day, especially in the late afternoon. The chances are that the fatigue mentioned above is due to hypoglycaemia, especially in the case of an alcoholic. However, it is possible that other factors are involved; hence I must stress the importance of consulting a doctor.

Hypoglycaemia (low blood sugar) can cause many discomforts. I will merely list the most frequent ones; my purpose is to help you ask questions concerning sugar, not to publish a treatise on hypoglycaemia, which is clearly beyond my competence. Among the discomforts caused by hypoglycaemia, those of which the alcoholics I know complain most often are: fatigue in the late afternoon—weak spells—anger, impatience, mood swings, outbursts, depression, need for prolonged sleep, negativism, personality changes, emotional instability, anxiety, anguish without apparent cause, headaches, migraines, suicidal thoughts and many more. It is important to realize that one may suffer from one or a few of these symptoms.

But since it is a case of "low blood sugar", why not merely increase the sugar consumption? Right. But it all depends on the type of sugar! Sugar in fruit, yes; the refined variety, like table sugar, no. Granulated, refined white sugar serves as a base for nearly all other sugars; it should be avoided by hypoglycaemics in particular, and by anyone who is concerned with following a well-balanced diet. If one feels tired—or feels some of the discomforts mentioned above—a glass of orange juice will work wonders. This natural fruit sugar is better metabolized on the cell level, and will not cause a drop in energy. The same applies to the sugar in vegetables, meat, fish, milk, cheese, eggs, nuts, in short, in all natural foods. Honey must also be avoided by hypoglycemics; it is not really "natural"; it is produced by bees and its sugar content is much too high. All syrups, including maple syrup, are likewise forbidden. The same goes for candies, chocolates, pastries, sodas containing sugar. According to some specialists, all types of carbohydrates may be taken in moderation; others prefer that they be excluded from one's diet: bread, pasta, potatoes, green peas, beans (used for making pork and beans) etc. Grapes and prunes are not recommended because of their high sugar content, and bananas because they are too rich in starch.

Coffee, tea and tobacco are also forbidden to hypoglycemics, hence to a good number of alcoholics! However, decaffeinated coffee and tea are authorized, as well as herbal teas. Another brochure, *Low Blood Sugar*, highly rcommends the spiritual principles of A.A. as a means to rehabilitation, and has this to say: "The members of A.A. are increasingly aware of their high blood sugar and the need for being treated. The coffee, sugar and countless cigarettes regularly consumed at A.A. meetings make abstinence rather difficult for its members..." This quotation generalizes a little too much; it might have been better to say that abstinence could perhaps be made more difficult for "certain" members. One thing is true: in a difficult situation, when anxiety levels are high, one should, as much as possible, avoid eating the foods we have mentioned; it's a good way of overcoming "stress".

Acute cases of hypoglycaemia may lead to coma, convulsions, schizophrenia, etc. but they are rare. However, I have known people who, after having eaten a chocolate bar or a large quantity of sweets, behaved exactly as if they were drunk: they had trouble walking, thinking straight and expressing themselves. One day, Roger, an A.A. member, was stopped for drunk driving. The Officer asked him if he had taken alcohol. He replied he hadn't taken a drink in five years. Neither had he taken medication of any kind. Finally, he was discharged on the statement of his doctor that Roger was in a diabetic coma. After a series of specific tests, Roger was diagnosed as suffering from serious hypoglycaemia; he was told that all types of artificial sugar were very harmful, and that, if he wished to stay healthy, he must follow a very strict diet. He felt tired and depressed all the time, and seemed to have lost the will to live. I knew of a clinic in Ottawa that specialized in hypoglycaemia, and since Roger was very anxious to get better, we made an appointment and spent several hours at the clinic. It was during this visit that I also took the tests. I can assure you that as long as Roger follows the doctor'instructions, he is very well; but if he strays... As for me, being an alcoholic, I am among the 80% mentioned above; but my hypoglycaemia is mild. If I indulge in sugar, pasta or coffee, I am overcome by a kind of fatigue, a weariness which I don't normally feel when I abstain.

Please to note that I have not exhausted the subject of hypoglycaemia. If you think you have a serious case of hypoglycaemia, consult a specialist. Hypoglycaemia may require more extensive, complex treatement, and as

164

I have said, your illness may arise from many other causes. Should you not wish to consult a doctor, and yet are a little worried or anxious for no apparent reason, and get angry for nothing, why not plan a healthy diet anyway? It can do you no harm; on the contrary, everybody should avoid certain foods, as well as tobacco. Give yourself one month; I guarantee that you'll feel like a new person.

It is possible that you found these pages on hypoglycaemia useless. However, countless people have told me that they found in them—along with the spiritual programme, of course—what they needed to lead healthy, peaceful lives. But there is a danger of which I am well aware: instead of seeking spirituality, one might be inclined to think that all one has to do to improve one's inner life is to follow the right diet. Well, we can't do much about that: some people will never be able to handle two things at the same time: steps and a healthy diet! We might as well try to find excuses for temper tantrums: "I can't help it, my blood sugar has dropped!" What can we do in the face of such lack of judgment? Go on hoping and loving.

To those who are tempted to cut down on what is detrimental to their well-being, here is a list of foods that are "allowed" and of those that are "forbidden":

Allowed:

All types of meat, fish, eggs, cheese, milk, cream, nuts, whole wheat bread (little); all broths and soups (except pea soup), oatmeal or soya (not other cereals), peanut butter. All vegetables except potatoes (few), green peas and beans (few). All fruit except grapes and prunes (few), too rich in sugar. No dates. Few bananas. All fruit juices, except grape, plum and prune (little). Decaffeinated coffee and tea. Herbal teas. Canned juices (sugarless).

Forbidden:

Potatoes (few), peas and beans (few), bread (little if it's whole wheat), all pasta, pastry—pies and pizzas —chips and other snacks.

Few grapes, plums, prunes. Few bananas. No dates. Little grape, plum, prune juice. No canned juices with added sugar. No coffee or tea except decaffeinated. Sodas.

Honey, syrups (including maple syrup), chocolate, candies, white sugar, brown sugar, pastries and cakes, jams, in short, everything containing refined sugar. All cereals except oatmeal and soya. Tobacco (cigarettes, pipe, cigars).

It is recommended that healthy snacks be taken in the middle of the morning and of the afternoon, as well as at bedtime (a fruit, a stalk of celery, a little cheese); this will help to maintain the appropriate level of sugar in the blood. Vitamins are also recommended, especially the B complex, including niacinamide, but we must remember that vitamins alone are not sufficient; a diet high in proteins but low in carbohydrates is essential.

In a serious case of hypoglycaemia, the doctor may have to forbid certain foods we have allowed above, prescribe medication, other vitamins, more minerals, and call for very specific tests. The information contained in this book is very general and is not meant to replace more thourough testing and a medical diagnosis, followed by prescribed treatment.

Envy and Jealousy

Envy makes us covet the happiness and advantages of others. **Jealousy** is a feeling of chagrin at the sight of the happiness and advantages of others (a form of self-pity).

When have I been—or am I—envious or jealous?

_____

Envious of the wealth of others?

_____

of their prestige? _____

of their culture? _____

of their physical appearance?_____

of their health? _____

of their popularity? _____

of their circle of friends? _____

of other things?

_____

Once again, we feel inferior. Our pride is wounded. We fear we won't be loved or admired as much as those who seem to be more advantaged than we are. Hence: PRIDE and FEAR (INSECURITY).

A Lover's jealousy

It's the fear that the person we love should become enamored of someone else. This type of jealousy is very painful for both parties—for the person who is jealous and for the partner: "Its motive may be real or imaginary, that is to say, the rival may really exist, or merely be imagined by the jealous party. If the latter is the case, then the jealous person is suffering from a personality disorder often associated to an inferiority complex. This is a completely self-centered individual, but at the same time, an anxious type. He loves himself above all. He doesn't necessarily love his partner (in fact, he may unconsciously hate her). He fears his personal value won't be acknowledged; very often, he will invent reasons for being jealous. Our cultural and social conventions provide him with excuses: passion and honour. But in reality, he is afraid of being rejected. He can only cure his jealousy by becoming oblivious of himself, through self-negation."

According to this quotation, the main causes of jealousy in love are self-centredness (egocentrism) and the fear of rejection. Once again, we see how much suffering can come from an **ego** totally wrapped up with itself (**pride** of a wounded **ego**), and from **fear**. If you have answered "yes" to the question: "Are you a jealous lover?", you would do well to refer to the section below on **selfishness**; I like to think that it will hearten you and give you hope. Do not despair: God has already accepted you and He understands you. Talking it over with someone in step five will begin to liberate you, and, through steps six and seven, God will do the rest.

Sadism

Instead of being saddened by the happiness of others, the sadist rejoices at their misfortunes. (Ask yourself if you are a sadist and answer in writing).

Avarice

Although this failing is not peculiar to alcoholics, it might be useful to examine ourselves on this point. Without actually being avaricious, we may occasionally be stingy or worry too much about the future. Skimping on the money we give our family, so as to have more to spend on ourselves, is not avarice, but selfishness. The avaricious person wants to hoard, not spend. (Ask yourself about this and answer in writing.)

Laziness

Avoidance of effort and work. **Laziness** should not be mistaken for **fatigue**, which can be the result of insomnia, overwork, etc. Some A.A. meetings may continue in a restaurant, which can be very pleasant indeed, but leave you feeling a bit under the weather the next day. Our eating habits may also bring on fatigue that we may mistake for laziness. (See **violence** and hypoglycaemia above.)

Gluttony and Drunkenness

Drunkenness does not concern alcoholics, alcoholism being an illness. Besides, we no longer drink. There is no point in going into all the fine distinctions here. Non-alcoholics can examine themselves and answer in writing.

As for gluttony, anyone can easily answer. Even if we don't acknowledge that we are greedy, we should remember that overeating can undermine our health, bring on fatigue, and lower our work output. (See **violence** above and hypoglycaemia.)

Finally, those who cannot refrain from overeating should consult O.A. (Overeaters Anonymous). They can surely help.

Lust

(Already dealt with in the sixth point of the moral inventory under the heading **sexual behavior**).

Selfishness

The selfish person always relates everything to himself. The opposite of selfishness is love of others in all its forms: altruism, devotion, selflessness, generosity.

Selfishness is not "willed" as such. It is a turning inwards, the defense mechanism of people who have been hurt and need to be loved a lot. Selfishness has its roots in a very demanding **ego** that becomes our one concern. It constantly conjugates the reflexive form of the verb to love: I love myself. We have not yet understood that this **ego** craves to be loved by others, not by itself. It's true that nothing is more important than to love ourselves, provided this love is the fruit of the love others have for us, of what their love teaches us about ourselves: "Since others love me so much, I must be loveable." That is why it is urgent that we "allow ourselves to be loved" by God first, and then by others, so that we may come to realize and to believe that we are worthy of their love. From this love, coming from God and neighbour, we shall, little by little, learn to accept ourselves as others accept us, to forgive ourselves as others forgive us, and to understand ourselves as others understand us. For this to happen, we have to establish bonds with persons whose human qualities and spiritual maturity make them able to accept others unconditionally; these persons love themselves, because they have known for a long time that they are loved by God and a few close people. The love of one person is not enough: even if he knew his wife loved him, a man could not very well conclude that he is lovable; doesn't he also wish for the love of his children, his brothers and sisters, his in-laws, his neighbours and friends? And when a man or a woman no longer believe in the love of those closest to them, only God's Love can save them. From that Source of Love, the love cycle can be regenerated: we come to love ourselves because we let God and others love us, and that in turn allows us to love others better. That is the law of love.

Our selfishness is proportionate to our lack of faith, for believing in God also means believing we are loved by Him. We try to compensate for our lack of faith and lack of love by showering praise upon ourselves, trying desperately to believe in ourselves. We begin where we should have ended: believing in oneself can only be the result of our faith in God and faith in others.

Am I too self-centered? _____

Do I "let God love me as I am"? _____

Can I truly believe that God loves me according to His Heart and not according to my merits? _____

Have I understood that only Love can transform my whole being, that the only way I can grow is in loving? Therefore I must let God love me. _____

When people show affection for me, am I capable of accepting that they are sincere, or am I inclined to believe they are just being polite? _____

Self-Centredness

It has the same roots as selfishness. The egocentric individual sees himself as the center of the universe; whatever happens to him is far more important than what happens to others: he wants all eyes to focus on him. He dramatizes everything, exclaims in horror at the slightest pretext, demands sympathy or praise... This type of behaviour is not willful unpleasantness: there is a lot of pain buried underneath. The remarks on selfishness apply here as well and, hopefully, will bring the same comfort.

Egotism

The egotist talks about himself incessantly; he is the only topic that ever interests him. He doubtless suffers a great deal from not being understood or listened to. Whatever the case may be, his **self** is dying to be loved. Do I, at meetings, have a tendency to talk of nothing but myself, for long periods of time? If your answer is yes, don't feel too badly about it, but rather be happy that you are aware of it. The aim of taking stock of our lives is not to arouse eternal regret, to cry or feel sad. Our sole intention is to discover what needs to be changed, with God's grace. We should picture that we are doing it sitting in a garden, amicably discussing with the Lord Jesus Himself what we wish Him to change in us. It should bring us joy: the joy of knowing that we are far from perfect, and that God will be only too happy, in the years ahead, to help us fulfill the best in us.

Finally, if we tend to go on about ourselves, it's a good idea, before meeting people, to make up our mind to inquire about their health, their children, their work; to ask them if they are interested in art, sports, travelling. You might just find someone who has the same tastes as you. It's very easy: people like to be asked about what they like.

Lying

(We shall consider three types.)

1. Lying to dazzle, to enhance oneself

Some people have such a low self-esteem that they feel they must magnify everything in order to be loved more. It's important to be caring and understanding with them, and not to upset them by calling them liars. The questions asked in the section on selfishness will most likely bring some comfort to them.

Do I, in order to be the focus of attention:

exaggerate the price of things? _____

call "friends" people I have met only once? _____

exaggerate events? _____

(Other questions.)

It isn't that this habit is very serious or harms others, but why not get used to being loved for what we are, rather than for what we own, or for whom we know? Let us make the resolution—when we think of it—to state things just as they are. We shall very soon find out if we are less loved. And if that is so, we don't need that kind of love!

2. Lying to exonerate ourselves, to shirk duties or obligations

Let us first establish a principle: you don't have to tell the truth about yourself to everybody. For example, an indiscreet person may ask you point blank the most unexpected questions: "Where do you work? How much do you make? Have you ever been in prison? Are you the faithful 'kind'?" You are not obliged to tell him the truth and can give any answer you wish. "Admitted to God, to ourselves, and to one other human being..." (Fifth step). It doesn't say: to the whole neighbourhood, nor to a room full of members!

Have I lied (or kept quiet) so as to let someone else carry the burden of my own misdeeds? _____

To avoid being caught? _____

To avoid being blamed? _____

(Lying or infidelity to one's spouse is analyzed in the following section.)

(Other questions.)

3. Lying out of insecurity in love or to hide infidelity

These questions might have been dealt with under the heading **sexual behavior**. If not, they may be answered here.

Has it always been easy to pretend that I really loved someone, when it was only a passing fancy? (The other might have thought you were serious, become attached and suffer as a consequence.)

If you have answered "Yes" to this question, **pride** may be at stake, as well as insecurity (**fear** of loneliness). Should real harm have been done, and if amends can be made, the name or names of the persons hurt must be added to the list in step eight.

Did I lie to my spouse to hide an affair? If such is the case, and if the spouse knows nothing of the affair, it's not wise to tell; it would merely cause unnecessary suffering, especially if the affair is over. If it's still going on, and you absolutely want to be considerate toward your spouse, don't you think the best thing to do is to call off the affair? However, if for the time being you can't bring yourself to do it, keep quiet: people don't have to be broken-hearted because of your sudden attack of honesty! To refrain from saying anything is the elegant solution, and shows more respect: "... except when to do so would injure them or others" (Ninth step).

You may add more questions on lying if you find it necessary.

False Witnessing

It's extremely serious and may be the cause of a wrongful conviction. It must have no place in our lives from now on. As for making amends for the past, where possible, the ninth step will offer suggestions.

Slander

To slander is to reveal misdeeds and faults that we know of in others with a malicious intent. Slander is the scourge of social life: I know very few people who don't take pleasure in revealing other people's faults, especially if they don't like them. How wonderful to bring them down, to laugh at their expense, while keeping the conversation going! It's all very sad! Rare are those who have never slandered. Why do we act so uncharitably toward people? We surely do it without thinking: what kind of human beings would we be if we did it on purpose? Deep in our hearts, I don't believe we really want to harm anyone. If we are customarily guilty of slander, let us ask God, with all the sincerity we can muster, to help us "think" before we speak ill, and I am certain we shall learn to keep whatever we know to ourselves.

Am I in the habit of slandering? If any harm has been done, and we can make amends, we'll see how in step nine.

Nota bene: In step five (confiding in another human being), we will tell our slanders, if necessary, but we must be very careful not to reveal any names; this would merely be more slandering.

Calumny

We can undermine someone's reputation by leveling false accusations against them. What we said above about slander applies to calumny.

Do I spread libelous accusations? Again, how to put right any harm we might have done will be discussed in step nine.

Theft

The answer should come easily; how to go about returning stolen goods, where possible, will be dealt with in step nine.

Fraud

The aim of writing anything down here is to **see**, **to acknowledge** that we are guilty of fraud, and not to compensate those we have defrauded. That will come in step nine.

Do I have a tendency to defraud? _____

Other types of criminal behaviour (rape, premeditated assault and battery, murder, death threats, etc.)

If we are guilty of one of these crimes (or any other), we must believe that God has forgiven us for our past sins, and turn resolutely to the future. If you have read and accepted everything we have said so far in this book, go in peace; God will grant you all the understanding and help you need. Believe me.

You can see about making amends in step nine. For the time being, it is enough to **see**, **acknowledge** and **confide** (step five).

Persecution Mania (could have been analyzed under the heading of SELF-PITY)

It takes the form of excessive touchiness and mistrust of others. "That was intended for me."—"Do you really think she gave me that to please me? It was meant to humiliate me!" etc. Ascribing twisted motives to others, without proof, shows a lack of generosity. Feeling someone is always out to get us, our Ego is constantly on the defensive (**pride** and **fear**). If you saw this fault in you when you were reflecting on **self-pity**, there is no need to answer again:

Do I tend to suspect others of wanting to exclude me, hurt me? etc. _____

Do I demand too much attention? _____

(Other questions if needed.)

Segregation

Refusing, rejecting, or excluding someone supposedly in the name of virtue, or some old bourgeois prejudice, or strait-laced morality. Our so-called "dignity" or "social rank", our "I cannot possibly, in view of my position, speak to such a person", are deemed valid excuses to justify a behavior that Jesus Himself condemned in the people at the Temple. Of course, we can't be expected to be close friends with everybody. But we do owe everybody respect and consideration, especially the members of A.A.

(If this applies, reflect on your behaviour and write down your findings.)

The Critical Mind

If it turns to "fault finding", it becomes a negative trait, but it is important to understand that, in itself, a critical mind is essential to good judgment. The **critical mind** examines everything carefully before accepting it as fact; it is the faculty that allows us to distinguish the true from the false. It implies level-headedness, and in this sense, the term is never pejorative. We could call it constructive criticism.

We should all strive to acquire a critical sense. Without it, we are no better than dupes and fools, unable to get a clear view of things. As far as A.A. is concerned, we should at least study the *Big Book* before marvelling at the first piece of rubbish that comes along, or rejecting as ridiculous an interesting and rich idea.

Tolerance does not mean that we should accept with equal grace the true and the false, the good and the bad, the sublime and the ridiculous. If we must tolerate the false, the bad and the ridiculous in our lives, we should at least be able to tell them apart. However, we should avoid personal attacks and fighting ideologies; we don't want to engage in arguments and controversial debates. Before accepting or rejecting a proposition, we would do well to consider it carefully. When asked for our opinion, we should present lucidly, with humility, but also with conviction, what we believe to be right.

Our critical sense is thus a useful tool. As such, it will allow us to rightly evaluate an idea, a sentence (always in context), a suggestion, a proposal made by a member or the group. But the person or group who made the suggestion should never be subjected to our attacks.

The Criticising Mind

The overly critical mind is looking for reasons to pass an unfavourable judgment, and dwells on mistakes, failures, reasons to doubt and suspect. The criticizing mind has a tendency to focus on people's faults; we could call it destructive criticism.

Are we not all more or less inclined to criticize others? This unfortunate tendency, if not eradicated, or at least controlled, may cause a lot more harm than we think. Destructive criticism, besides serving no useful purpose, denotes a lack of education. It nearly always goes beyond the merely unpleasant and becomes slanderous.

Am I inclined to constantly find fault with others? _____

Am I prepared, in the future, to focus on what is good, generous and real in the persons I meet? _____

Intolerance

A feeling of animosity, of resentment, even hatred, for people who do not think as we do. It may result in "clans" of those who are for and those against. This is both futile and harmful, especially within A.A., where no one works as a professional, but where each member tries to offer generously the very best of himself. We certainly don't have to share a member's point of view, but it's quite another thing to resent him and to want to harm him for it. Fortunately, intolerance rarely goes that far.

Am I intolerant to any degree? _____

Do I lobby against what others think? _____

Do I think I am entitled to "straighten them out"? _____

Am I, deep down, something of a dictator? _____

Purity of Intention

Acting without ulterior motive. It's not always the case; for example, people marry for love... but it helps if the future spouse is also wealthy. To sponsor someone because... well, it's tempting. To work... for prestige. To visit an aunt... in view of her will.

Within Alcoholics Anonymous, we must be honest and true. Some members may exercise a certain influence; they should never seek the prestige that comes with it. In passing, may I remind you that sobriety is a gift of God. The sponsor is but His servant, the instrument, the spokesman of the spiritual message of A.A.

Are my intentions always pure, devoid of ulterior motives:

When I attend a meeting? _____

When I accept to be a sponsor? _____

When I make friends? _____

(Other questions.)

Could it be that I see certain people because of their money? their social position? However, it is possible that we struck up a friendship with people for their money and position at first, and that, with time, the relationship developed into a sincere and durable friendship.

The Question of Money

We are not talking about greed here, but about the race for money, the amassing of material goods for the prestige they bring (if not with the hope of buying love). And it may very well happen that you are loved because of your money.

The whole question of money is not an idle one. It is fundamental, essential, of prime importance. Although the saying: "Money doesn't bring happiness" is well known, we persist in believing that somehow money can. Alas, money brings comfort, but not happiness, which has its source elsewhere.

It goes without saying that we need money to live. So be it, provided we don't live for money. It does, no doubt, alleviate many a suffering, and contributes to extraordinary human achievements. However, it's unrealistic to think that those are the usual goals pursued by people with money. One would have to be naive to believe that.

Money is the most dangerous of masters; it enslaves those who serve him. "No man can serve two masters; for either he will hate the one and love the other, or he will be devoted to the one and despise the other. You cannot serve God and Money." (Mt. 6:24) Think of the quarrels, the hatred that money breeds, the break-ups that it causes! So many worries, energies, fears, so much pain, weariness and despair, all for money! We may not have reached that point yet, but we have to keep a close eye on ourselves, and reflect on the question of money, so that, little by little, we may become more detached. It isn't easy, and for some, it will take a long time. Money can bring a false sense of security which very often lulls us into believing that we have no need of God. "Again I tell you, it is easier for a camel to go through the eye of a needle than for a rich man to enter the kingdom of God." (Mt. 19:24) And it won't be God who makes it difficult to enter, but the rich themselves, self-sufficient as they are, who have no use for the things of the Kingdom. Too busy with their own affairs, they can't see why they should enter this celebrated Kingdom only to be bored to death!

Let us mentally take stock of all the things we have bought, thinking they would make us happier. We will soon realize that, apart from the essentials, we have accumulated an impressive number of objects that have long stopped giving us pleasure and merely clutter our lives.

The more we live by spiritual values, the less we worry about money; it is inescapable: "...he will be devoted to one and despise the other..." Nothing could be more true! How many alcoholics decided to join A.A. when they were completely—or almost—broke! And it was there they finally met God. Let us ask God, in our prayers, for the health and strength necessary to earn our living, and at the same time, let us consent, with Him, to become detached from material possessions. We will thus be able to own things without being owned by them, so that, if some day we should lose them, we won't be too unhappy.

Am I inclined to believe that material goods would bring me happiness? _____

Am I engaged in the race to make money? _____

Am I so concerned with money that I forget other values? _____

Have I quarrelled with family and friends on account of money? _____

(Other questions.)

On the other hand, am I aware of the importance of earning a living for myself and my family? _____

Am I prepared to reimburse the money I borrow? _____

Let's have no illusions: it's not easy to live detached from material possessions. Just because we have admitted being attached to money and things, and we have talked it over with someone (fifth step), we can't expect to be liberated on the spot from their hold on us. We shall need God's help and it will take time, but we will be free as we progressively make room for the Kingdom within us.

Human Love

No moral assessment would be complete without serious reflection on human love, the one true love everyone seeks. In point six, we have studied behaviour related to love, in particular sexual behaviour; but what I wish to speak of here is that senseless, irrational hope we cherish, the hope of finding in human love perfect happiness and the ultimate fulfilment of our dreams. We are not bigots, and are not shocked by the slightest hint of an affair, nor would we wish to moralize at all costs. Besides, true morality recognizes behaviour most likely to generate true and lasting happiness. Would people be happier if they gave free rein to their thoughts of murder, theft, violence, jealousy, or hatred? We would all have to shut ourselves in our houses, and we could hardly talk of a happy society. Therefore, it all comes down to knowing if the great love you are living now— or wish you were—is as great a guarantee of happiness as you imagine it is. If your love is true, affectionate, lasting, then you are blessed, and may you enjoy every minute of it. We would like to extend the same wishes to the whole world.

However, if we look around us—also at A.A. which we know quite well—we see so many broken hearts, so many desperate, lost souls, frantically searching for the great love! This is not a reproach; it seems that the whole world is love sick. We expect far too much from human love. Many are happy only when basking in human love. Should this love waver, their joy is threatened; if it dies, their happiness falls apart. But only illusory joys fade; the true ones are eternal. To search desperately for the one true love is strangely reminiscent of our quest for God. To wish for human love is one thing; to search desperately for it, and to be unable to experience hope or happiness without it is quite another. I have already discussed this in the preceding chapters; if I bring it up again is so that self-awareness can begin through the moral assessment.

It is very frustrating and painful to persist in seeking happiness in human love, and never to find it. We sometimes categorize people: "He chases anything in a skirt...", "He just wants a good time... "She plays around with men". To talk in this fashion is to know very little about the human heart. Neither he nor she are having much fun; they are, in fact, suffering. They are both searching for true, lasting love, affection and understanding, kindness and peace. But something always seems to go wrong. Boredom sets in, loneliness comes back, and they secretly begin to hope for something else. Why? It's hard to say. Part of it is doubtlessly due to a lack of maturity. Whatever the case may be, my aim is not to give a course on true human love, and I doubt very much that all the books written on the subject would alleviate the pain of not knowing true love. Everybody knows that passion is not the only means of union between man and woman: friendship, understanding, mutual respect, mutual devotion are far more stable and lasting. However, knowledge does not make us more apt to find love, nor more capable of living it.

If you are among those who search for love and fail to find it, or those who are constantly disappointed in love; if you feel alone, isolated, on occasion even desperate, turn to God: He is the Source of all Love; He is the one true **love**. Reread the beginning of this book, and pay special attention to the parts dealing with love.

The same basic reflections apply here

Keep telling yourself and believe that God loves us, as we are, with all our deficiencies, as if He would love someone who has been hurt.

Turn to others and help them. Those who do not belong to A.A.—or some other similar association—could offer their services to their priest or pastor, or to some charitable organization. There is much to do for the sick, the infirm, the elderly...

Accept the love given by the people you help. If you only knew how the sick and the elderly look forward to your visits, and how much the members of A.A. love their sponsors.

Understand that it will take time—in some cases years —to change, and while waiting, learn to accept yourself as God accepts you. (To accept does not mean "to approve". To accept, for God, means to understand and stand by, to encourage us to go a little further on the way to becoming our better selves. God is always beckoning us to reach beyond ourselves.)

Some points you may have missed

The moral inventory is now complete. Some may have scruples about having forgotten something. No need. When taking stock of our lives, we can only see ourselves at a given moment. If later we should discover some fault we overlooked, we can analyze it then (the tenth step will provide help) and we can talk it over with someone at the appropriate time. That's all there is to it.

I shall close by quoting from the *Big Book*: "In this book, you have read in several places that faith enables us to do for ourselves what we were incapable of doing alone. We hope you are now convinced that God can help you overcome your individual will that has kept you apart from Him. If you have already made up your mind, and if you have taken stock of your main faults, it's a good start. You have swallowed and digested large mouthfuls of truth concerning yourself."

Very important: you will need your sheets for the fifth step. Keep them in a safe place where no one who might be hurt by reading them can find them. If necessary, use code words for names; be very careful. Some will want to destroy their written inventory immediately after having confided in another in step five. It isn't a bad idea, provided you keep a copy of the names of all the persons whom you have harmed in word or deed, through anger, jealousy, slander, calumny, lies, debts, theft, fraud, etc... without forgetting the names put down in the third point of the inventory, concerning the harm caused against those you resent. This precaution will save you having to make the list all over again in the eighth step. "Made a list of all the persons we have harmed..." Why not recopy these names right now? As you are in the right frame of mind for this type of work, it would only take a minute, and it would be done once and for all. We shall now go on to step five: "Admitted to (...) another..."

Part six

CONFIDING IN ANOTHER

Admitted to God, to ourselves, and to another human being
the exact nature of our wrongs.
Big Book

A.A. members are quite familiar with the notion of confiding in another human being. Even if you are not a member of A.A. (or of a similar association), you would greatly benefit from such a practice. Friends of mine learned to abide by the twelve principles of A.A., and have every reason to congratulate themselves for having followed this spiritual "methodology".

What Does It Consist of Exactly?

In the course of our moral assessment, we have often called on God. It is in His company we have done all this work, ever conscious of His presence and His encouragement. Having carried out our search in an atmosphere of friendship with God, we were able "to see" our deficiencies without anguish, shame or guilt. On the contrary, we felt pleased at having had the courage to look at ourselves and admit that we were far from perfect. We realized that God had given us the grace to do so, when so many refuse to "look at themselves".

It is now easy to collect our thoughts in the presence of God, as in a prayer, to go over everything we wrote down and to "admit to God", as well as "to ourselves", what we have discovered. We bask in the same warm affection that we would have felt had we spoken to Christ in person while He was on earth. We are not being sentimental: Christ lives, and He promised to be with us until the end of time. Now that we have completed our self-evaluation, we can truly commune with God, undisturbed by cerebral pursuits. Our prayer —and praying is talking, and conversing—now takes place at a more intimate level. Once we have reached this point, what remains to be done is to take our notes and share them with someone. But let us first consider the following points :

— In whom should we confide?

— Why should we confide in someone?

— Make an appointment and abide by certain rules.

— A word of advice for "the listener".

— The outcome of confiding in someone.

In Whom Should We Confide?

Generally, the members of A.A. confide in their sponsor, but it is not always the case. It often happens that a sponsor, chosen at the outset, and with whom we maintain strong ties, is not the person with whom we wish to journey spiritually. This may seem contradictory because the sponsor, in principle, should initiate the newcomer to each of the twelve steps. However, because of his personality, his presence, his openness, the sponsor may remain the ideal friend with whom we love to share our daily life, but, because of a different concept of God, or a different type of spirituality, we may prefer to consult a person who seems closer to our inner needs. Whatever the reason, the choice of the person in whom to confide is entirely free. It doesn't even have to be a member, just "another human being..." A friend, a priest, an uncle, it doesn't matter, as long as you trust them. Without it being absolutely necessary, it's better to find someone who understands the spiritual aspect of this step. "It is important that it be a person who can keep a secret, who understands clearly and approves what we are trying to do, and who doesn't try to change our plans."

Why should we confide in someone else?

Why indeed, some will ask? Isn't it enough to confide in God? First of all, Alcoholics Anonymous does not share that view : "Admitted to God, to ourselves and to another human being..." You will find A.A.'s arguments on this in their *Big Book* . Here are some more points.

In the first place, telling someone else takes the drama out of things. When someone says : "I can't even talk about it", they are in fact saying that it's too personal, too awful, too secret. After all, modesty and decency demand that we refrain from revealing certain things. And so, whatever is deemed too awful to be revealed remains inside, a frightful secret we would rather not think about. This is called repression. If we could overcome our apprehension and "say" what we thought "impossible to say", we would no longer dramatize, since that "impossible to say" thing would now be "said"! That is because speech emanates from an extremely high level of consciousness—the exclusive domain of man—and the simple fact of putting something into words, instead of "repressing" it in the depths of our being, lifts us to the highest level of consciousness possible. These points may help to dispel our fear of "saying" and sharing personal things.

In the second place, we do not have the monopoly on understanding, acceptance, forbearance and common sense. To someone who is embarrassed about revealing something very personal, we say most encouragingly: "Come on, you can tell me anything! I wasn't born yesterday! I have lived long enough to see my share of things! Believe me, I can understand. And you don't have to worry; I won't breathe a word to a living soul. Go on!" This is our attitude :"we" understand. But how is it that, when it's our turn to tell, there is no human being on earth generous enough, or understanding enough to deserve our trust? That's nonsense, of course. There are, all around us, sensitive and kind-hearted people who have suffered a great deal and who, having carried the weight of their own lives and of their own sins, are now capable of helping you carry yours, with kindness and understanding. You are not alone. Seek and you shall find. Ask God for guidance.

In the third place, we don't offend God in the abstract, but in our fellow man right next to us ! Just as I cannot serve God except by serving my fellow man, I can only offend Him when I offend another human being. That is why we must turn to God and to others. We have hurt human beings; it is now to another human being we must turn. Of that we can be sure.

Finally, we must confide in another human being to enjoy a little of God's kindness here on earth. I remember as though it were yesterday—and yet, it was eighteen years ago—the day I opened my heart to my friend Robert. Although he was not an A.A. member, I chose to confide in this good, kind man whose wife was a childhood friend. Nurtured on their deep faith in God, both of them understood very well the meaning of this encounter. I was expected. Gisèle had prepared coffee, and I was greeted with the kind of emotion that marks special occasions. She had withdrawn discreetly almost immediately, while her husband showed me into his study, closing the door behind us.

I was not the least bit anxious, but I did feel a little nervous. I asked God to be with me, and without further ado, with my sheets in hand, I began to speak. Robert listened in silence, except for a few words of approval to let me know that he was following. Never did he show the slightest expression of surprise or disapproving gesture; he gave me his full attention in a friendly, brotherly manner; his face lit up from time to time with a gentle smile. It is on a human face that one best sees God, and I have never seen Him as clearly as on Robert's. God is friendship, and tender love with a simple, gentle smile. And it is this love that He has put in Robert's heart, in Gisèle's, in yours, in mine.

When I had finished, Robert shared his impressions with me: "I am edified, he said; I wonder if I could confide in someone like that. It's quite extraordinary!" Following this meeting, Gisèle and Robert decided to put into practice the twelve step program, including "Confiding in another", which neither of them found that hard. Do you want to experience how sweet it is to open one's heart to God's Love? Confide in a kind friend. Do you wish to see God's face? Gaze at the face of someone you love. Gazing at faces will teach you about love. Look at the wrinkles on your mother's hands and face; you will see love. Glance at a visitor's greying temples; you will know patience. If you look beyond the faces, you will learn to see God. Don't hesitate any longer; take your sheets of paper and run... to find a face to love!

Make an Appointment and Set a Specific Time Limit

Setting up meetings between A.A. members, and spending several hours on the fifth step does not usually present any problems. Remember, however, that several hours devoted to listening may cause fatigue; it requires stamina. And don't make the mistake of thinking that one hour will be enough to tell everything about yourself; it may take between three and five hours. If you have written down your inventory, and stick to the text, you will finish well within this time limit. In some rare cases, the confiding took up to ten hours. Often the listener doesn't dare express his fatigue for fear of hurting the other party. On the other hand, it is understandable that the one talking hopes to finish in one sitting and has no desire to come back another day. It took a lot of courage, in the first place, to undertake this process and it would seem tedious to stop and start again. So be methodical. Stick to your text as closely as possible so as not to waste time. But don't rush through it either: this step is important for you; it is essential to take all the time you need, but without too many details and digressions. Once again, between A.A. members and close friends, it is always possible to find a way.

However, and this happens frequently, things can go quite differently with someone you don't know as well. For example, you might choose to confide in a priest, a nun you knew long ago, a teacher you once had, your family doctor. If they can't give you more than a couple of hours at a time, you may well have to plan two meetings with them. Whatever you decide to do, make the appointment, specify its duration and stick to the plan. During the meeting, keep track of the time yourself, so that your listener won't have to remind you when it's over.

One last recommendation: the person you have chosen to confide in may never have participated in this kind of exercise, and may not know what it involves in terms of time and concentration. After four hours of intense listening, they may be tired. Take this into account and let them know in advance so that they may plan their schedule accordingly.

A Word of Advice for the "Listener"

If you have never been a "listener" in someone's fifth step, and you are asked to be, it isn't very complicated. You don't have to do much except be encouraging, understanding, kindly accepting. The person you are receiving will no doubt be a little nervous; for them, it's an important step, and a difficult one without a doubt: telling the most intimate details of one's life can be a very emotional experience. If it's a member of A.A., have plenty of coffee ready. Avoid interruptions, comings and goings; choose a quiet, out-of-the-way room.

Abstain as much as possible from answering the phone. In short, everything must concur to creating a peaceful setting for someone who will be experiencing inner turmoil. Finally, as I have already mentioned, set aside a few hours. If you see that you are beginning to get tired, say so and suggest a break of fifteen or thirty minutes; you can then resume the meeting refreshed. I am often asked if, when listening to a fifth step, it is necessary to talk, to give advice, etc. Personally, I don't think so. The person has not come to consult you, but to be listened to, to "tell their story". Knowing how to listen is more important than counselling. However, if the visitor starts feeling remorseful and unhappy, soothing words of encouragement will be needed. Let your heart be your guide. If you create an atmosphere of acceptance and affection, the right words will come to you when you need them.

When everything is over, you will have lived an experience very much out of the ordinary. Since becoming a member of Alcoholics Anonymous, I have listened on many an occasion to a fifth step, and yet, even after all these years, I am always in wonder and awe before the person who is speaking. Indeed, what an amazing thing to see someone trying hard to explain his mistakes, to watch him follow on his sheets hours of work spent in acknowledging them; to witness the effort he is making —and it isn't easy—to be as objective and as sincere as possible. What grandeur there is in this search for the truth! I always feel so small in their presence. How could you possibly not love, with all your heart, someone struggling to admit, with a lump in his throat, that he was wrong? Then you will understand how much God loves the one who admits his mistakes, how fondly He accepts him, how happily He forgives him. You will know better what divine Love is.

The Outcome of Confiding in Someone

There is no doubt that, after having finished the fifth step, one is light-hearted, happy and free. As I said above, one is bound to feel apprehensive about revealing the most intimate part of oneself, and no one looks forward to this step. If one considers all the work that went into the fourth step, and the effort and nervousness of having to talk about it, it's no wonder that one feels delighted and relieved to have such a great weight off one's mind!

But there is more to it, much more. First, we are very happy to have fulfilled two of the requirements of the A.A. program, which brings to five, instead of three, the number of steps taken. That in itself is important. Then, we have lived a spiritual experience: through the listener's acceptance, understanding and kindness, we have had a taste of God's love for us. Finally, we have succeeded in putting into words what had always seemed impossible to reveal. We have thus taken the drama out of a part of our life we certainly can't be proud of, but over which we shall no longer make ourselves sick; after all, when we told our listener, he didn't have a fit! We have also understood that our mistakes, our misdeeds are not the work of a monster, but the work of man. And men will be men (women too, for that matter!) I will end on a quotation from the *Big Book* of Alcoholics Anonymous concerning the outcome of the fifth step: "Once we have fulfilled this requirement, not having kept anything back, we are delighted.

We can look the world in the eye. We can be alone and yet comfortable and at peace. Our fears have been dispelled. We begin to sense the closeness of our Creator. We may have had certain religious beliefs in the past, but now, we are beginning to go through a spiritual experience. We will often have the impression that our alcohol problem has disappeared. We are convinced of being on the wide road, walking hand in hand with the spirit of the universe."

It doesn't say that we were liberated from our character defects or our failings, neither that we are transformed. We have admitted our wrongs, our faults and shortcomings to someone; that is a lot, but not all. We cannot, strictly on our own, be transformed as we hope. Our transformation will come from God, which takes us to the sixth and seventh steps.

Part seven

COUNT ON GOD ALONE
RATHER THAN ON YOURSELF
TO MAKE THE BEST IN YOU
SHINE THROUGH

*We have fully consented to let God remove our defects of
character. We have humbly asked Him to make our
shortcomings disappear.*
Big Book

God! He is the hearvester, the Master of the vineyard,
the worker who can bring out all the potential within us.

Indeed, we must understand—just as we did for our
alcoholism—that we are absolutely incapable of ridding
ourselves of our defects of character and our deficiencies. What we are facing are not just superficial traits,
but deeply-rooted "defects of character", as well as
"deficiencies", in other words, "that which we lack".
Our transformation can only come from God, and we
must fully consent to let Him work through us. Are you
God? Certainly not. Then why do you work so hard to
overcome your deficiencies? Of course, we would very
much like to come before God "brand new"! "Here I
am, O Lord, I succeeded; aren't You pleased with me?"

It would doubtless be more flattering to be proud of ourselves than of God. It bears repeating: only someone better than ourselves, not our equal, can help us improve. We have no choice: we shall have to consent to let God eradicate our defects.

Does that mean there is nothing for us to do? Certainly not: what I meant was that we must redirect our efforts. For example, didn't we do our utmost to overcome our alcohol problem? We started by keeping track of the number of drinks; then, we said to ourselves that beer alone couldn't do any harm; then, we tried drinking only with meals; finally, we decided to stop drinking altogether, but to no avail; sooner or later, we would start again. But isn't it normal that we should try this way, for the sake of our spouse, of our children? Unfortunately, nothing worked. So, what did we do?

We stopped thinking that we could win the battle against alcohol; we accepted defeat, and that was a terrible source of anguish and despair. But, from the depths of our misery, we came to believe that God—and only God—could help us. In His infinite goodness, he led us to Alcoholics Anonymous, and we were made to feel welcome there. And that's when we redirected our efforts: instead of waging alone a losing battle against alcohol, we accepted to attend meetings, we listened and learned, we put ourselves in God's hands, we continued to pray, we served others, we transmitted the A.A. message, in short, we did only those things we could manage, and we did them joyfully. Believe it or not, we stopped being thirsy! While we were busy doing these other things, God Himself took care of our alcohol problem, to the point that we didn't even think about drinking.

The explanation lies in the fact that we are not "just alcoholics"; we have other dimensions to our personality; it isn't because we are alcoholics—or in a wheelchair for that matter—that we are incapable of devotion, understanding and acceptance. On the contrary, it is in alcoholism itself, in our own weakness, in this very evil that we find a gift of life for another alcoholic who is dying. Our mission is born out of our deficiency: God can always turn our suffering to some good. Did He not guarantee our resurrection from our death? And were we not reborn inside after an evil had destroyed us?

In our moral assessment, we have acknowledged, it is true, our deficiencies and faults; but we must never think "that we are only that". We are not only pride, anger, jealousy, slander, calumny; we are also capable of being truth, gentleness, affection, devotion, warmth and understanding. In other words, there will always be in us a little bit of the opposite quality, or of the opposite defect. Who can boast—even if he be a saint—of being perfectly humble, perfectly kind? By the same token, who can claim to be totally devoid of honesty or goodness? Who, for example, can stay angry twenty-four hours a day, every day of his life? Every force in us has a positive and a negative pole. The most effective, and pleasant, way to weaken the negative is to accentuate the positive.

One cannot "work" on a defect or a deficiency (negative force) any more than one can "work" on a fire. The thing to do is to get its opposite: water. It is useless to try and fight hunger as such; it's better to concentrate on finding "what is lacking": food (positive force).

Instead of trying to overcome a tendency to anger, we should apply ourselves to developing what we lack in our character: gentleness. This may seem naive. What is the difference between "I won't get angry anymore" and "I am going to try to be gentle"? Same thing? Not at all. The first resolution can only apply on specific occasions, the second may be practiced all the time. In order to put into practice "I won't get angry anymore", someone has to hurt or insult you. If you are quick-tempered, chances are that you will give in to anger. Your deficiency is being put to the test, and not having worked on becoming gentler, you can only fall back on your resolution not to get angry. Furthermore, this happens at a tense moment, whereas God is calm and harmony. But couldn't God make a "direct intervention" and help us not to get angry? I don't think so, no more than He intervened "directly" in our alcohol problem when we didn't do anything more than "wishing to stop drinking". God suggests that we act: we joined A.A. and we devoted ourselves to others.

The opportunies to practice gentleness are numerous and not confrontational: visiting the sick, welcoming a new A.A. member, spreading the message, organizing an anniversary party, encouraging a newcomer, telling him how much God loves him and how much you love him; all these are much more pleasant and effective ways of becoming gentler that waiting for someone to provoke our anger so that we can practise "not getting angry"! Let's live what is positive in us and that will force the negative to recede.

To trust in God means above all to trust in Him to sanctify us, to make us better. We cannot do it alone; better to cultivate the good in us, leaving it to God to deal with the bad: "Deliver us from evil... while we try to do all the good of which we are capable". Nothing is gained by wasting time and energy making "efforts to improve our character". If you have a tree in your yard, do you go out every morning to see if pulling at it will make it grow? It grows on its own. So it is of the Kingdom in us. And He said to them: "The Kingdom of God is as if a man sowed a seed in the ground: whether he sleeps or rises, night and day, the seed sprouts and grows, he knows not how. The earth produces of itself, first the blade, then the ear, than the full grain in the ear." (Mark 4: 26-28)

To accept that our transformation will come slowly but surely, to believe that our shortcomings will never entirely disappear, and to count on God for our growth, that is humility. "Humbly asked Him..." But being humble doesn't mean to grovel before God—that's silly —but to expect everything from Him instead of from us. Being humble is accepting to be loved, without a fuss, in all simplicity, like a child. To be humble is accepting that God loves us as we are. Finally, to be humble means accepting to be poor.

It is when the association of Alcoholics Anonymous was able to convince alcoholics the world over that God would love them as they were that they opened up to life!

The therapeutic value of the Gospel lies in detachment and self-negation, in order to minister to others; it is the criterion of the Last Judgment: "Inasmuch as you have done unto the least of my brethren..." It is understood that to get rid of our deficiencies, we can't just stand there and "do nothing". If we were to add up, for the last twenty years with A.A., the countless hours spent passing on the message, attending regular meetings, conventions, anniversaries, study sessions, listening to someone on the phone, at home, in a restaurant, in a car; all the energy given to organizing, planning, meeting, explaining, welcoming, understanding, encouraging, sympathizing, we would come up with an impressive total. Yet these years went by like a dream, as if there was nothing to it. Because, you see, through it all, I lived the joy and the enthusiasm of love! If I mentioned the work that we accomplished, it wasn't in any way to complain, or to brag. I have long since been rewarded. It was simply to show that we didn't "just stand there, doing nothing", and to emphasize that, if God is willing to transform us, we must be willing to become workers in His vineyard.

But there remains for us to give our **full consent** to God, so that He may remove our faults. It may take a long time before we **fully consent** to let go of a particular habit, to become detached from material goods, to distance ourselves from certain people. We are afraid to find it too painful, to be left alone, powerless and bored. Tell me, did you find it hard not to drink today? You didn't, did you? Yet there was a day when the very thought of it would have made you literally ill. God is Kindness itself; that is why He took away your very desire to drink, and now, there is no pain involved. It will work in the same way with your deficiencies, but it will take time, often a long time. How many years did it take you to fully consent that God help you to stop drinking? How many years do you think it will take you to consent to His help in all the other areas of your life? That is the question.

It is quite normal to hesitate, and to give God only partial consent to our transformation; we are so terribly afraid to suffer. Of course, we proclaim our consent, in words... But, deep inside, are we not tempted to pray, like Augustin: "My God... take it, but not just yet"? "If we are attached to something we don't want to give up, let us ask God to give us the willpower to do so." (*Big*

Book). Since God does not coerce our will, it might be a long process in some areas. But let's not get discouraged; detachment will come eventually, with time and good will.

When it comes to our character flaws and our deficiencies, even with our **full consent** to God, we won't be transformed overnigh. The comparison with our alcohol problem bears repeating: we may have been able to stop drinking from one day to the next, but it will take the rest of our lives to bring out, little by little, the best in ourselves, and we shall die without having succeeded, because living is "becoming". Who can unequivocally state, on his death bed, that he is perfect?

Time is of the essence. God waited forty years for the Jews to cross the desert, a distance which, today, can be covered by car in one day. Our personal experience corroborates the fact that it takes time to change. We trust in God's grace to improve ourselves, but we must patiently accept that it will take time. And the waiting is difficult to bear. Who has not wished to be totally liberated after a few weeks of prayer? Disappointment was bound to follow. I do not doubt that some may have undergone, like Saint Paul, a sudden, shattering transformation. But that is not the general rule. Wanting to go too fast on our spiritual journey prevents us from accepting ourselves as we are at any given moment along the way. To love someone, as God loves us, is to accept him "as he is" and not "as we would wish him to be". And that is the whole point: to love and accept oneself.

Carl Rogers makes a very interesting point: "Yet, the paradoxical aspect of my experience is that, the more I am willing to be myself in all the complexities of life, and the more I am willing to understand and accept the realities in myself and in others, the more changes occur.

It is indeed paradoxical that, inasmuch as each one of us is willing to be himself, he will find, not only that he is changing, but that those people around him with whom he is involved are also changing. That is certainly the most striking aspect of my experience, and it is also one of the most profound lessons I have learned in my personal as well as in my professional life."

To consent to change, **to wish** to change is good; **to want to change at any price** is an obstacle to our progress, because it implies that we do not love ourselves here and now, that God is not pleased with us here and now. It is also placing conditions on loving ourselves and on the Love that God bears us; and since acceptance, of God's Love for us and of what we are, is the driving force of our spiritual progress, we impede it from the start. **To wish** to change does not imply "that I don't like myself where I am", and, conversely, "to accept myself as I am" does not imply "that I am so stupid as to fail to understand that I should change". Carl Rogers has this to say about the meaning of loving oneself: "It isn't bragging or a way of imposing myself, but rather the peaceful satisfaction of being myself".

I wish to change, to become better, more open to God and others, but I do not make that a condition for accepting myself, for loving myself as I am. "You will love your neighbour as yourself", that is to say: you will love others inasmuch as you are able to love yourself. God too loves me as I am. He wishes me to change, to improve, to become more open to His Love and to the love of others, but He does not make this a condition of His Love for me. The starting point of a spiritual journey is accepting to be loved by God for no reason at all, like the poor. We absolutely must believe in this Love, whoever we are, wherever we are, no matter how lost we are. For Love is God. And since we trust in God for our spiritual growth, how can we possibly move forward if we do not believe in His love for us, such as we are? Not believing that God loves us here and now, spontaneously, amounts to not believing in Him at all, since the Love God bears us and God Himself are one and the same: God is Love.

For the very reason that God loves us as we are, He will be happy to make us move forward. That is why we must also love and accept ourselves as we are, at any given moment, not to interfere with God's love for us, guiding us on our spiritual path.

"So, we often worry, God approves of everything we do, good or bad?" I didn't say that; I said God loves us as we are, whatever we are. To Love is not necessarily to approve; it bears repeating again and again. Do you approve of everything your children do, especially in their twenties? Are you in favour of all their ideas, their follies, their mistakes? But I know very well that in your heart, you love them dearly as they are, whatever they may do. And it's because you love them that you refrain from trying to impose your will on them, with insults and threats; it's because you love them that you respect their freedom, their right to go their own way. You know very well that they will grow through their suffering. And even if you tried to use force to spare them pain, they would think all along that they could have found happiness exactly where you forbade them to go. It's not easy to love. Do you think it's any easier to be the God of Love? Why do you think the Father had to sacrifice His Beloved Son for us?

I think the answer lies in the fact that God has more faith in us that we have in Him. It is because God believes in us that we believe in Him; could our faith come from anywhere else? God has absolute faith in our ability to change, to improve, in our potential for good. And it is when we consent to respond to this loving and patient hope the Father has placed in each one of us that we begin to believe in ourselves, to hope for ourselves, in other words, to consent to change. To love someone is to believe in him, to believe that, in spite of everything, the very best of him will shine through one day. To stop hoping is to stop loving: "You will always be the same; you will never change." When we no longer expect anything from ourselves, when we no longer hope in our ability to change, we no longer love ourselves.

It is illusive to want to become better thinking that God will love us more for it: it's quite the opposite! We don't become better "so that God will love us", but "because He loves us" and transforms us with His Love. It's believing in His Love that makes us better. We are not loved more today than yesterday: only yesterday's Love could have made us grow. Not being prone to our emotional instability, God has always loved us, with the same intensity, the same affection, the same hope: we shall never be loved more than we were in the past, nor more than we are loved today.

We often despair of ourselves. Sometimes it seems that, in certain areas, we are making no progress or, even worse, that we may not have what it takes. We can barely get going: how can we hope to move ahead? We must keep believing and hoping. In the case of some members I sponsored, I hoped for so long, wanting so much to believe that their best would surface, that with time it did.

It isn't because we don't see or don't feel the potential in us that it isn't there. Would you tell a mother that her newborn won't have teeth because you can't see them?

She wouldn't believe you! Because this newborn is the son of man, we know he will have teeth. In Christ, we are all brothers and sisters, sons and daughters of God. Potentially, we sport all His Colours. If Jesus believed and hoped in us to the point of dying for us, if He offered us the Kingdom, it's because He knew each one of us was capable of growing.

Part eight

MAKING AMENDS

Made a list of all persons we had harmed, and became willing to make amends to them all.
Eight step

Made direct amends to such people wherever possible, except when to do so would injure them or others.
Ninth step

In step eight, we find the resolve to make amends; this will be carried out in step nine when we make up for our wrongs. It's important to understand that this resolve to make amends entails a much greater commitment on our part than merely to "acknowledge our wrongs and ask to be forgiven". The expression cleary means to redress a wrong and compensate for it, wherever possible. Finally, in this step, we are concerned with those "we had harmed", in other words, persons to whom we have caused **real harm**, serious worries or pain. It is certainly proper to apologize to someone with whom we have been unpleasant in the past; but being unpleasant is not really a "wrong" in the strict sense of the word. Therefore, if the opportunity arises, an apology is sufficient, but we don't have to go out of our way to meet that person.

Drawing up a List of the Persons We Have Harmed

All we have to do is copy the names we have already listed in our written moral inventory—the name of those we have harmed because of resentment, anger, jealousy, slander, lies and infidelities, theft, fraud, unpaid debts, etc.—Wrongs committed since the completion of the original list will naturally have to be added.

Should you no longer have the written inventory and wish to proceed to step eight, you can do one of two things: use the questionnaire below, or for more details, refer to Part Five of this book. Here then is a guide line to help you draw up a list of the persons you have seriously wronged.

Before beginning our task, let us remember that we are no longer alone. God is with us and He understands: His role is not to condemn, but to encourage, support and strengthen us by His understanding and His affection. God does not hold us back with reproaches; He wants us to better ourselves and is there to show us the way. If our hearts are open to His Love and Forgiveness, the past will be forgotten; knowing that we are capable of growing, God will look to the future. Let us now begin our task in peace and confidence.

Because of **pride** (wounded self-image, touchiness, vanity) and **fear** (insecurity, jealousy, envy, money problems)—which only a great love could have alleviated—we felt frustrated, bitter and, out of resentment, we often hurt others deeply. In some cases, we even sought revenge and tried to harm them. However, it may well be that we caused some wrongs quite unintentionally. For instance, the problems we might have caused when we were drinking, before we knew A.A.. I am thinking also of all those words we said without think-

212

ing, all the rash judgments we made, our happy-go-lucky attitude, our recklessness, our lack of experience, our ignorance: ignorance of real values, and of the Kingdom within us. I do not seek to excuse such behaviour. That would preclude the good will to make amends by refusing to acknowledge our responsibility. Instead, I am trying to understand, to accept... to love. If, when consulting the table of contents of this book, you had decided to tackle first the "list of all persons we had harmed", I must urge you to read the preceding chapters first. They might gently prepare you for the task that lies ahead: looking inwardly.

Let us begin our list of those to whom we have caused real harm, worry or pain:

I. Because of anger, resentment, intolerance, jealousy (at home, at work, with our relatives, our acquaintances, at A.A.)

A. In words:

  1. Slander and calumny: (names) _____

  2. False witnessing: (names) _____

  3. Shouting insults: (names) _____

  4. Threats: (names) _____

  5. Caustic or petty criticism; harsh judgments; mockery, contempt, insinuations: (names)
    _____

B. With silence (ignoring, sulking, being absent):

  1. Refusing to talk, ignoring someone out of resentment: (names) _____

2. Refusing to greet, to shake hands, to speak (in public) etc.: (names) _____

3. Staying away from home for a long time without sending news out of revenge, sulking: (names)

_____

4. Refusing to invite, to receive (out of resentment): (names) _____

5. Refusing invitations from: (names) _____

6. Others: (name) _____

C. In deeds:

1. Physical injuries: (names) _____

2. Threats of assault: (names) _____

3. Death threats: (names) _____

4. Night disturbances: (names) _____

5. Damage to property out of revenge: (names)

_____

6. Rejection, segregation: (names) _____

II. By infidelity to one's spouse:

Lying, in the sense of keeping something from one's spouse, does not have its place here. Infidelity is a lie in itself, but it is better not to tell the truth to one's spouse, under the pretext of "total honesty"; it would only cause more pain, do more harm. "...But we can't reveal to our spouses or our parents what would hurt them or make them unhappy. We do not have the right to save our skin at the expense of another. We shall tell this part of our life to someone who will understand, but will not be affected. The rule is to be hard on ourselves, but considerate to others" (*Big Book*).

1. Have we been selfish, dishonest, thoughtless?

   _____

2. Have we aroused, without justification, jealousy, suspicions, bitterness, sorrow?_____

3. Who else may have been hurt? (children, parents, friends, etc.) _____

III. Theft: (names of individuals and firms)_____

IV. Fraud: (names of individuals and firms)_____

V. Other ways of causing harm, damages: (names)

   _____

VI. Money questions:

1. Refusing, out of resentment or selfishness—although we had the means—to provide for our family: _____

2. Refusing, out of resentment or selfishness—although we had the means—a certain luxury to our spouse or family: _____

3. Refusing, out of resentment or selfishness—although we had the means—to pay alimony or child support: _____

4. Failing to care about our debts; not making arrangements to pay even minimal weekly or monthly instalments: _____

5. Other thoughts concerning money: _____

The preceding questionnaire covers just about all the possibilities of hurting, harming or doing someone wrong; but it's only a model: you may add to it whatever you deem necessary.

Once the list is done, step eight is completed if we have made the firm resolution to make amends "directly" to all these persons *wherever possible, except when to do so would injure them or others.* The parts in italics need some explanation, after which we may proceed to making amends.

First, why make amends for our wrongs? To punish ourselves, to learn how to live? Not at all! We must do it because it's only fair, and also to grow, so that we may become honorable men and women. It is a difficult step, one that often requires a lot of our time. Whatever the case may be, it is nobler to make amends than to allow others to bear the consequences. Suppose you find your parked car has been damaged; you will have infinitely more respect for the person who leaves a card than for the one who sneaks away. Further arguments would be superfluous. Making amends often calls for great courage; God will not refuse it to those who ask.

Making amends "directly" applies when we know the persons well, especially if they are members of the family; it is important that we approach those we have hurt or wronged personally and in private. Sometimes at a meeting of Alcoholics Anonymous, someone having to address the meeting takes the opportunity to make amends to his or her spouse sitting in the room. This gesture is well-meant, but it does not fulfil the requirement of making amends "directly". It is relatively easy to apologize in public; it's much more difficult to sit down in private with the person concerned, to admit to him or her one's wrongs, express regret and ask for forgiveness. Very often, we avoid this kind of encounter for fear of bursting into tears. Emotions are difficult to control. Don't forget that this step is the ninth; we have come far on our journey, and should thus be better equipped to deal with it.

However, in certain specific situations, making amends directly may be avoided. Suppose someone wanted to return stolen money. Knowing himself to be hated by the injured party, and being familiar with the latter's vindictive nature, he is convinced that to approach him directly would only cause more trouble, in spite of his good will. In this case, a third party could return the money on his behalf without revealing his identity. A priest or a minister would serve very well in this capacity, as their usual duties give them the credibility and discretion required in this transaction. If in doubt as to the best way to go about it, especially if loved ones are involved, we should seek counsel with one, two, or even three trustworthy persons. Prayer will also help. If we are in good faith, and truly wish to make amends, we'll find solutions.

"Wherever possible": clearly, no one is ever called upon to do the impossible. But we'll have to be very honest with ourselves and not declare impossible what is merely difficult. If a wrong cannot be totally redressed, it may be redressed partially. Each one must answer for himself. We often hear: "I no longer drink, my behavior has vastly improved, everybody can see that; that's good enough." Allow me to differ. Not to drink is the least we can do "for ourselves" when we are alcoholic, and the world doesn't have to be dumbfounded by it. Even if we think we are exempt from apologizing, the harm we have done still needs to be put right.

"Except when to do so would *injure them* or others."
A typical case would be that of a married man (or woman) who has had affairs, and whose spouse has remained loyal and faithful. If the latter is unaware of it, confessing would merely cause useless suffering. I have already dealt with this case previously, and will not repeat myself.

If we should meet someone who has done more harm to us than we have done to them, we strictly adhere to our side of the blame without discussing theirs. This type of encounter calls for great strength and it is important to wait until we are ready for it: there are seven steps to be completed before the eighth and ninth steps which we are now discussing.

In the case of debts, especially sizable ones, arrangements should be made as soon as possible. Too often, people wait to be able to pay back what they owe in one lump sum, and so they put off indefinitely their duty to reimburse their debts. In general, no one will refuse regular instalments. It is important to make a start.

If someone were to refuse to see us, there is nothing we can do; we certainly aren't going to break down their door! Perhaps a little later... If, on the other hand, having agreed to meet us, someone treats us harshly and reproachfully, we mentally turn to God and pray that He help us to accept. But this rarely happens. Nearly always —if not always—the most difficult people will be deeply touched by our sincerity and will show signs of friendship. As we move ahead with making amends, we shall be liberated and find new happiness. We will not regret the past, but neither will we forget it. We shall understand the meaning of serenity and know peace. No matter how low we sank, we shall see how our experience may benefit others. Feelings of futility and self-pity will disappear and we shall become more interested in our companions. Selfishness will vanish. Our attitudes and our way of looking at life will change completely. We shall no longer fear people, or economic insecurity. We shall know intuitively how to handle situations which previously baffled us. We shall suddenly realize that God is doing for us what we were unable to do for ourselves.

Does this sound like wishful thinking? I don't think so. It is happening among us, sometimes very fast, sometimes slowly. And it will continue to happen if we work in that direction.

Could anyone wish for more?

Part nine

THE DAILY INVENTORY

*Continued to take personal inventory
and when we were wrong, promptly admitted it.*
Big Book

Reflecting, every night, on the quality of our thoughts, our words, and our actions during that day.

It's a simple and pleasant way of making progress, and it only takes a few minutes. Did I hurt anyone today? Did I cause pain? Was my thinking positive and enthusiastic? Did I avoid self-pity, vain regrets, useless worrying and resentment? If we can honestly answer favorably to these questions, we shall experience a feeling of well-being. On the other hand, if we find ourselves at fault, we will at least have the satisfaction of realizing it. How many top executives, professionals, financiers, political leaders, all very much aware of their importance..., how many go to the trouble of doing this?

Through a daily self-examination, we will avoid slipping unconsciously into selfishness, dishonesty, resentment, fear, and everything else that inhibits the manifestation of the best in ourselves, in short, into all that keeps us out of the range of love, acceptance, tenderness and peace. We know that we are capable of growth. As I said, taking daily stock of ourselves is simple and requires little time; the difficulty is to remember doing it! As long as we don't develop the habit, it's easy to forget and to let the weeks, months, and years go by without ever giving it a thought.

Besides weighing our faults and shortcomings, the daily inventory also provides the opportunity—and that is much more productive—of becoming aware of our successes, our progress, our growth. Nothing is more conducive to staying in God's arms than to realize that, through Him, our wonderful world has begun to flower, our tree is bearing fruit, and we are continuing to grow. Some A.A. friends, although trusting in the Father, have confided to me that they often have the impression of being at a standstill. I always tell them that it's because they don't see themselves moving forward day by day: "Are you sure that, since you came to A.A., you have made no progress?" "Good God, of course I have! I am not at all the same person!" Don't say that you are standing still. You are just not taking the trouble to watch yourself grow.

However, if we don't see growth in certain areas, it's equally true that we fail to notice that other areas are receding. It's not good will, courage or love that are lacking: we just don't see all that we have accomplished because we don't take stock of ourselves. And that is a shame.

Finally—this is my personal experience—among those who have encountered God and put themselves in His hands, I don't know of anyone who has failed to achieve progress. Nevertheless, the daily assessment will double the rate of growth, and the fact that you are aware of it will make you persevere in joy.

Here is a simple way to proceed every night:

1. Did I hurt anyone today?

   — By what I said (criticism, insults, unpleasant or sarcastic remarks, etc.)

   — By my attitudes (sulking, keeping away, silence, failure to listen, etc.)

We shall often be happy to find that we have hurt no one in the course of the day, and that, on the contrary, we have listened to, encouraged and consoled others. We may have spent the evening with a new member, or in passing on the A.A. message. The day was thus filled with kind and beneficial words. It is extremely important, even essential to our growth, that we be aware of it.

If, on the other hand, we were impatient, malicious, angry, we can still do something about it: we can ask those we have hurt to forgive us. If we find that hard, we pray for courage.

2. Did I cause anybody harm today?

   — in words (slander, calumny, mockery, etc.)

   — in deeds (dishonesty, theft, fraud, blows, etc.)

I don't know you, but I doubt you spend all your time harming others. You will find, as we all do, that you are not a monster, and that, if you have wronged someone, you are not so hard-hearted that you don't regret it. So ask God to enlighten you on the best way to make amends as soon as possible.

But most of the time, you will be delighted to discover how helpful you were: picking up a member, planning a meeting or an anniversary, visiting a sick person, doing someone a favour, etc. That's how we discover our generosity, our capacity for giving without ulterior motive. This awareness plays a large part in building the self because it reveals the beauty of what we are. It is a fact that people do more good than bad; rarely is a whole life spent causing others trouble. At any rate, that would soon become impossible in a life given over to God.

I included the *Daily Inventory* in this part of the book for reasons of convenience. Since I have dealt above with the more elaborate inventory concerning wrongs to others, the daily inventory should be easier to understand. Why not make it a daily practice right after we have gone through the step of confiding in someone? There is no reason to postpone it.

Going over our day every night will afford us moments of pure joy and an opportunity for self-love, since we will realize that, in spite of everything, we are ready to serve, to listen to, understand and accept others. Is there a better way of sanctifying ourselves? Let us do this and we shall live. As for our character faults or deficiencies, the Father will see to it that the negative in us recedes, as He teaches us, day by day, to let the best in us break through. Let us remember: the beauty of what we are is in our future.

Part ten

SERVING GOD BY SERVING OTHERS

Having had a spiritual awakening as a result of these steps, we tried to carry this message to alcoholics, and to practise these principles in all our affairs.
Big Book

Indeed, through our years with Christ, many of us have experienced a Love that we have tried to communicate to those who suffer, to all "the poor". Personally, I have not stopped at passing on the message of God's Love to alcoholics only; other friends of mine, and they are many, feeling alone and isolated, were able to benefit from the message and have put into practice the requirements of the program.

What Message?

"We tried to carry **this message**..." It should be clear that the message is contained in the eleven preceding steps. In the light of the chapters already read, the message can be expressed as follows:

— That we came to understand that there is no human solution to our loneliness and our isolation, no human answer to our need to be loved...

— How we came to believe that only an Infinite, Divine, Supernatural Love could reach us in the depths of our heart...

— Which way of seeing God became for us the best answer to our excessive need to be loved...

— Why and how we should make a moral assessment of our lives and why we need to "tell another"...

— That, having understood that God alone can transform us, make us grow, we came to rely wholly on Him, rather than on ourselves...

— That we had acknowledged our wrongs and tried to make amends, as far as possible...

— How, each night, we assess our day, rejoicing in our good deeds, while promising to apologize or make amends for any wrongs committed...

— How we consent, through prayer and meditation, to leave it entirely up to God to guide us in our search for happiness, and to give us the courage needed to go on living...

That is the message this book brings to you. However, one need not have completed the entire journey before being able to show the way, nor must one wait until the eleventh step before experiencing a spiritual awakening.

It is certainly possible to show the way even as one is moving through the steps. Hence a newcomer to A.A. may let others know about the association, tell them what it is all about, share his hopes and his conviction on what he has undertaken, etc. But if he goes no further, he won't have anything more to share of the program. But if he deals with the question of God, if the encounter with Him takes place and the new member entrusts his life to Him, he will then be able to explain how he took steps two and three. It is possible to share our journey with others with each step we take, to help them to the point we have reached, no further.

As for "spiritual awakening", the term is used in step twelve, but that doesn't mean that it only happens then; all the steps contribute to our spiritual growth. "Having had a spiritual awakening as a result of these steps (the eleven preceding steps)..." In my humble opinion, the most startling moment of awakening occurs in the first step. Isn't it always suffering beyond explanation or consolation, an incurable wound, a limit we have reached, an insatiable need for love which open the gates of the Kingdom? This must be what entering the Kingdom through the narrow gate is all about. That's because suffering rids us of so many of our pretensions, while opening our eyes to the infinite value of our inner selves; we make ourselves small, not in the sense that we reject what we are, but rather that we become like children who understand at last that only the Father can help them grow. This committing ourselves to the Father, prayer, as well as all the other steps will widen the way, making the journey easier to a spiritual experience.

To pass on the message, one must of course find the occasion. In A.A., or other similar associations, there is no lack of opportunities: alcoholics requiring help, newcomers or members at other stages, anyone needing guidance on his way. Those who don't belong to A.A. won't have any trouble finding among their friends or acquaintances lonely persons, unhappy in varying degrees, persons searching for the meaning of life, of suffering, thirsting for a happiness they can't even name. But even then, I don't believe you will find enough of them. That's why it is also suggested that we visit the sick, the infirm, the elderly, prisoners, etc. and offer our services on a regular and permanent basis. To stop would mean to regress.

One way or the other, we must turn to others and minister to their needs; I can never stress this point enough. Encountering God, entrusting our lives to Him and praying are not sufficient. One must reach out to others. **The God of love is not an abstract theory**; to grow, to attain fulfilment and happiness, we must **live** our love. God is best served in the service of others. A true, evangelical spirituality puts us necessarily at the service of others. Hope for growth without service is vain.

Attending A.A. (or other) meetings is imperative; they are the setting for sharing and working, a place of acceptance and giving, an opportunity for making new friends, a time of service. Generally, A.A. members are happy to attend the meetings and they participate with joy. Does this mean that we have to go every night? It all depends on each one's obligations; a person living alone has more time than a father or a mother with five children. Clearly, spouses need to consent to their partner's spending many evenings at A.A. meetings rather than in other activities, especially if it seems very important to them. However, after a while, a balance should be maintained between A.A. activities and family time. I should like to talk about this in more detail as this question of balance is very much of a problem for some.

I have known alcoholics who could never become involved in A.A., either because they failed to recognize its importance, or because their family milieu did not favour attendance at meetings or was downright hostile to it, or yet again because their center of interest was somewhere else.

The importance, not only of attending meetings, but of being involved in A.A., is such that even with the most wonderful therapy, an alcoholic has very little chance of overcoming his problem if he stays home. Since alcoholism can't be cured, therapy must be continuous and permanent: once an alcoholic, always an alcoholic. There is a way for an alcoholic to live happily without drinking: to stay in an environment favorable to abstinence.

A fortnight ago, I was talking to an intelligent alcoholic who, I know, understands the scope of his problem, and has also accepted God in his life. Yet he was in despair because he had gone back to drinking. He had known A.A. for nineteen years, but after attending meetings for a few months, he thought that was enough, that he had understood; so he went back to his other interests and activities: his house, his garden, fishing, hobbies; all these things, he felt, would keep him away from the tavern. And there he was again. This time, however, he has the firm resolve never to quit his A.A. activities. If he sticks to his resolution and follows the steps, he will succeed.

Others, the intellectual type, hope to succeed by resorting to study, reading, the arts (where "the other" is not), to the point of doing just enough A.A. to keep them within the bounds of safety. They don't drink, but they are neither happy nor fulfilled: they give little, and receive little in return.

Finally, there are those who have to constantly defend and justify to their families their attendance at meetings, so that they grow tired of fighting and give up. Of course, they are wrong. But certain temperaments tend to be subjugated by family demands. If it wishes them to quit drinking, their family will have to love them enough to allow them to benefit from everything that A.A. has to offer. Everyone will gain from it. Otherwise, if they go back to drinking, everyone will lose.

I am, however, perfectly aware that some A.A. members of long standing tend to overdo it by spending an inordinate number of evenings at meetings, including Saturdays and Sundays. This may be a sign of poor judgment, but not always. It could be that, feeling uneasy inside, they depend too much on the meetings for their well-being. One would have to see if they have integrated deep spiritual values into their lives, if their family milieu is a congenial one... Hard to say. But I do know one thing: the best thing is for the non-alcoholic spouse to join the Al-Anon Movement to also create an accepting and giving environment, to find a place for work, for sharing, for making friends and serving. Under the pretext that they don't have an alcoholic problem, too many people believe that they can live without spiritual values, that they have no need of being fulfilled and that they can very well dispense from serving others. Somehow, sewing, gardening, fishing, the children, hobbies, will work wonders. And while their spouses at A.A. are making new friends, becoming someone special for somebody, the years go by. The non-alcoholic spouse remains the outsider, having nothing to do with the partner' joy. So many good times can be shared by the Al-Anon member and the A.A. member: anniversaries, open house, conventions, study sessions, etc. One and the other see themselves as equally useful, exchanging their ideas and plans. Furthermore, and this is not the least achievement, the joy of growing together spiritually and of following the progress of members sponsored by one or the other contribute to strenghten this common endeavour which can only open onto Life.

Why couldn't it be so for those who don't belong to A.A. (or another association) and who still wish to devote themselves to good deeds, as we have already said? It's better for both partners to get involved, to live the experience as a couple, so that both will share its joys.

Having said this on balancing A.A. activities and family life, I believe that if true spiritual values are integrated in one's life, each one will find the answer on how to harmonize personal and social life with the demands of A.A.

But if encountering God, entrusting our life to Him, and prayer do not suffice, neither do service and devotion to others. In order to grow spiritually, one cannot go without the other. If faith without works is not a living faith, conversely works without faith are an empty shell. Caring for the sick and the infirm is not the only way to attain fulfilment; they are not an end in themselves, but only a means. The end is God. Many nurses give the sick excellent care; it cannot be concluded that they are living a spiritual life on the strength of this observation alone. You must have heard the story of the millionaire who visited a leper-house in China. As he watched a nun dressing a leper's wounds, he said to her: "I wouldn't do that for a million dollars." And she answered: "Neither would I."

The same applies to A.A.; God must inspire our giving. It isn't enough that, in transmitting the message, we tell the story of our life and of our struggle with alcohol: "Appeals on the basis of emotion are rarely successful. The message which will be of interest to alcoholics must have weight and depth. In nearly all cases, the ideals presented must be rooted in a power superior to the wretches asking for help, if they are going to bring them back to life". And one must not make the mistake of thinking that making coffee, lining up chairs, chairing a meeting or doing secretarial work will in themselves promote our spiritual life and therefore lead us to sobriety **if one is alcoholic**. I am not saying that all these activities are not wonderful, useful, beneficial—there is nothing better to overcome shyness and lack of self-confidence—I am saying that these activities alone are not enough and that much more is needed: the practice of the A.A. steps is essential. And first among them, finding God, and then serving Him in others: "Truly, I say to you, as you did it to one of the least of my brethren, you did it to me." (Mt 25 : 40) To believe we serve God when we serve others, we must first believe in God.

Once more: at certain times of his life, an alcoholic has no effective means of mentally defending himself against that first glass. With very few exceptions, neither he nor any other human being can provide a defense. It must come from a Superior Power.

Offering the Very Best of Ourselves

Several persons have told me that, after a while, they start finding meetings boring. Perhaps it's because they continue to go looking to get something instead of going to give. Clearly, if we are not asked to speak, to read the steps or to thank, we could easily believe that we have nothing to offer. Not everyone can be asked to make the coffee, to chair the meeting, to take the minutes... What then can you give? The most important gift: **you**! Before going to a meeting, decide that you will speak to as many people as possible—it's in people's faces that we can best see God—that you will smile to them, inquire about their health, tell them how happy you are to meet them. All you have to do is say something nice and positive, give praise and encouragement. Tell a new member that you are excited about his arrival and certain that things will turn out beautifully for him. Avoid discouraging words or negative remarks, for they are the opposite of love's way, and hence of God. Listen more than you will talk, receive more complaints than you will utter:

> Complaining is a useless activity and one which keeps you from living your life productively. It encourages self-pity and impedes all attemps to give and receive expressions of love. Moreover, it reduces your chances of improving your relationships and increasing social intercourse... If you genuinely love yourself, complaining in front of people who can do nothing for you is absurd and indefensible.

Presenting a problem to one's sponsor, to friends or to persons who can help you is one thing, but complaining incessantly, with the sole purpose of attracting attention and pity is quite another. People may listen to you for a while, but soon they will start avoiding you. Stop complaining about your problems; apply yourself to solving them instead, and mention them only to people who can truly help you. Bill W. himself, at the end of a study session held during a Convention in 1955, wishing to underline the importance of giving rather than receiving, recited the beautiful prayer attributed to St. Francis of Assisi:

Lord, may I never seek so much to be consoled as to console,
To be understood as to understand,
To be loved as to love with all my soul.
It is in giving to all men that we receive,
And in forgetting ourselves that we find true riches,
And in dying that we're born to eternal life.

This attitude of "giving rather than receiving" can be lived anywhere: at home, at a reception, at work. Very often, we keep it for A.A. meetings, or for persons whom we want to help directly, and we neglect to offer the very best of ourselves with a simple smile, at home, at a restaurant, at a mall, anywhere in fact. A couple of weeks ago, I was present at a reception that brought together some hundred and fifty friends of long standing. I happened to notice three persons who stood out, in sharp contrast to the rest in their attitudes of listening and giving: they never once mentioned themselves or their concerns, but complimented everyone they met, expressing joy at meeting them and asking all kinds of questions about them, encouraging them to speak.

At the slightest mention of happiness or success, their faces lit up with approval, but saddened with compassion when told of misfortune. Their whole being was present to the other. This attitude indicates that a good distance has been covered in the individual's spiritual journey; a beginner can't be expected to possess it at the outset. On the contrary, he will be the focus of all the attention that the more experienced members are capable of giving.

Therefore, it would be a wonderful idea to develop the habit, before getting home, of collecting our thoughts for a moment and preparing mentally to offer our very best; to resolve to listen, to understand, to encourage, to praise. And as we said, we should do this before entering the office, the bank, the restaurant, the supermarket, before joining friends, wherever we have to talk to people. However, it will take much more than the perusal of these lines or a promise to ourselves to learn to do it. We have often repeated that to love, we need more than the will to love; we need to feel we are loved. But it's also true that we often miss the opportunity to love because we have failed to connect our hearts and our minds to the vital source of Love. We must keep trying. At first, we shall quickly forget the resolution we have just made. But if we persevere, we shall soon realize that progress is possible. Whatever happens, it's an interesting and charming wager with ourselves that we can make every time we meet someone. What can we lose when betting the best of ourselves?

Sponsorship

Sponsorship offers, without a doubt, the most wonderful opportunity for openness and self-sacrifice. The sponsor is at the member'side, so to speak, encouraging and guiding him, not only at meetings, but also on the spiritual journey of the twelve steps. Those who are not members of A.A. could also "sponsor" by showing someone the way. They will listen and provide encouragement, which is excellent in itself, but doesn't provide an answer to the problem that concerns us here. And it is precisely when we have no more answers to give that a spiritual solution would be more readily accepted, because it would come to fill a void.

Sponsorship is a more intimate presence, with a more specific direction. This book is an example. With someone whose heart has consented to turn to Christ, all that is needed is to humbly speak of one's own progression, without imposing it in any way, leaving the other free to accept or reject it, at his pace, in his own time; what he seems to refuse today, he might accept tomorrow.

To sponsor also means to bring the other to love himself, that is to believe in the best in himself, by constantly calling attention to the beauty he bears within, by making him aware of his generosity, his goodwill, his capacity for giving, in short, of all the best in him. And this will be achieved, not only by telling him, but especially by accepting him and loving him as he is, where he is, because that is what he needs. This love is vital to him, if we wish to see him grow. Realizing that he is loved and trusted, he will begin to believe in his own personal worth, he will begin to love himself. Regardless of the haughty, proud, pretentious attitude he puts on, a defeated alcoholic has ceased to love himself, to believe that he is any good. He is crushed. The last thing he needs is to be crushed even further. It's going to take all the love we can muster to save him.

Personally, I don't believe in techniques which aim at "crushing" the alcoholic in order to cut down his ego to size. That would mean creating a false, artificial base which would not be the alcoholic's own. What **he believes himself to be** is totally unworthy: he urgently needs to be lifted, so that he no longer has to resort to drugs to forget it. The first step in Alcoholics Anonymous deals with our personal limits when it comes to "doing" and "acting": the alcoholic acknowledges that he cannot solve his alcohol problem and that he can no longer cope with family, professional or social obligations. He may also be aware that he has "done" stupid things, and talked "nonsense", but he instinctively refuses self-condemnation because he knows very well that he **is not** what he **does**. That is probably why he reacts so strongly to harsh criticism of his behaviour. The *Big Book* of A.A. says: "We admitted we were powerless over alcohol—that our lives had become unmanageable." It doesn't say: we have admitted that we were pig-headed, proud, selfish, swollen heads! Of course, when making the moral inventory, we will become aware of our pride, selfishness, and many other things; but this assessment offers no solution; it invites us to go further. The solution is to entrust our lives to the Father, a Father who loves us unconditionally "where we are" and "as we are". The immediate solution: Love! The person who is ill must be confounded, surprised, astonished, stunned with Love, not struck, crushed and overwhelmed with unpleasant, arrogant, haughty remarks. Here is a very convincing Carl Rogers again:

We know that if the therapist adopts toward his client an inner attitude of respect, one of total acceptance of what he is, and of faith in his client's potential capacity for solving his own problems; that if these attitudes are suffused with sufficient warmth to be transformed into a deep sympathy and affection for the essential person of his client, and if then a level of communication is arrived at where the client perceives that the therapist understands his feelings and accepts them, we may be certain that the therapeutic process has begun.

I should like to comment on the following: "and faith in his client's potential capacity for solving his own problems". We know that an alcoholic will never find "on his own" or "in himself alone" the answer to his problem. This answer will come from a Superior Power. However, it is "on his own" that he will join Alcoholics Anonymous, and it is "in himself" that he will accept a God of Love; all he needs is for someone to show him the way... and to set out on it.

A Spiritual, Supernatural, Divine Solution

A.A. offers a spiritual, supernatural, and divine solution within a framework of totally free acceptance, brotherhood, and love. No more, no less. If you believe in the confrontational approach, there are specialists, psychologists and psychiatrists, who are trained in handling such techniques. Nevertheless, let me quote Dr. Arie den Breeijen, psychiatrist at Lakeland Psychiatric Center in Florida, whom I saw during a trip to Florida; at the time, I had already been a member of A.A. for twelve years. "We put the alcoholic back on his feet physically, and then we use all the arguments at our disposal to make him realize that what he needs is Alcoholics Anonymous. At the hospital, went on Dr. den Breeijen, we have set up A.A. meetings where we send our alcoholics, and the results are amazing. If we had to invent a technique for alcoholics, we would have to reinvent A.A. But what would be the point of that, added the Doctor, since A.A. already exists?"

Alcoholics Anonymous has clearly demonstrated to the world—in more than one hundred countries—what unconditional acceptance could do for alcoholics. And that, without any training other than suffering lived and shared in love.

Learning to Live Only Twenty-four Hours at a Time

Everybody can benefit from this very sound principle: live one day at a time. This "twenty-four hour" principle, very dear to Alcoholics Anonymous, did not originate with the Association. My maternal grandfather, who died in 1935 (the year of the founding of A.A.) used to say repeatedly that if one lived for today, tomorrow would take care of itself... that was his leitmotiv. And indeed, of what use can possibly be eternally regretting the past? Can it change it in any way? Can our fear of the future have any bearing on events? So, why not simply live today to the fullest? It's an intelligent, rational principle; anyone will agree to that. To a new A.A. member, for whom it is impossible to conceive spending the rest of his life without drinking, we explain that his commitment is only for "today", that tomorrow, he can always change his mind... The next day, he again commits for "one day only", and so on. This works for a while, until he has shaken off his obsession with alcohol. The liberation will come when he puts into practice the spiritual principles of the twelve steps. These constitute the A.A. rehabilitation program, which has irrefutably proven its effectiveness: one million alcoholics throughout the world, now living in a state of happy and relaxed sobriety thanks to A.A. are no figment of the imagination. Some might be tempted to say that statistics don't prove anything. All the same, they point to general trends. It's true that some members of A.A. never free themselves from their obsession with alcohol. But their number represents a very small minority compared to those who succeed; they are exceptions to the rule: "We have rarely seen a member fully engaged in our A.A. program fail." It's not always clear why these rare cases fail, but we do know why most succeed: it's thanks to A.A.'s twelve step program, and those who agree with me are legion. As far as I am concerned, I am quite glad at the thought that, for the rest of my life—were it to last a hundred years—I can do without a drop of alcohol: good riddance! I can't very well imagine myself repeating forever: "For today only"; it's just too tiring, difficult, unbearable. If you are among those who find it painful to abstain from alcohol, and you still have to consider it for only twenty-four hours at a time, don't despair; open your heart to God and soon—it is my most sincere wish for you—you will be liberated. Attend as many meetings as possible, turn to others, find ways of helping others, and most of all, believe that God loves you and is there for you; your obsession will disappear... on condition that you know what you want. "The only condition required for becoming an A.A. member is the desire to stop drinking." This "desire" is sufficient "to become a member", but to become liberated to the point of no longer being thirsty and no longer thinking of drinking alcohol, this "desire" must become "sincere, authentic, loyal" and be accompanied by a solid, firm decision, devoid of any mental reservation to the effect that "perhaps some day I could drink again". It is easy, with God's help, to stop drinking, on the condition that "we will it absolutely". Because, if your sincere desire is "to continue", you may be sure that God will not interfere with your freedom to do so.

However, "to live only twenty-four hours at a time" remains a principle like any other, for what it's worth, nothing more, and to which we should not attach the value of a step in the spiritual program. It's easy enough to live a day at a time when everything is going smoothly; but to a wife who has just been abandoned, to a desperate father who doesn't know if his child will live, to all those who are dying of boredom and loneliness, to those obsessed by their past who can't think of anything else, to all who suffer and weep, to those who have lost the will to live, we shall have to offer something more than "one day at a time". We shall have to teach the new member by what values to live his life during those difficult twenty-four hours, and how he can, little by little, a day at a time, integrate the spiritual programme of A.A.; how he can learn, a day at a time, to entrust himself to the Father, to turn to others more and more... All that, twenty-four hours at a time. For, you see, one can crave alcohol twenty-four hours at a time; one can feel isolated twenty-four hours at a time... all one's life! I remember Jean de la Chaussée d'Antin, a member from Paris, who quipped: "Before undertaking the spiritual program of the twelve steps, for two years, I was bored stiff at A.A. twenty-four hours at a time!"

Presenting the principle of "twenty-four hours at a time" without reasonable explanations can often produce the opposite effect to what is hoped for. A friend of mine, who had accompanied me to an open meeting, was very much impressed by the idea of "taking one day at a time". That evening, the chairman of the meeting, the secretary, the guest speaker had all introduced themselves as alcoholics "admitted and accepted for today only". To top it off, the recipient of his thirteenth anniversary cake had also declared: "Twenty-four hours at a time, my dear friends, and we get there." My friend leaned over to tell me: "How wonderful! What

241

willpower! Thirteen years, day after day, each morning having to start all over again! I can't get over it, she added, how hard that must have been! I take my hat off to him." Now, I knew that was not the message this member was trying to get across. He was merely trying to encourage newcomers by telling them that thirteen years seemed to be a long time... but that it hadn't been that long, since it was only really lived in periods of twenty-four hours, and that hadn't been so hard. My friend, however, had had the opposite impression. I may be wrong, but I don't think that the repetition of "... admitted and accepted for today only" and "twenty-four hours at a time" will offer promises of happiness to the newcomer. These clichés leave a bitter taste and have more to do with stoicism than serenity. No wonder that so many outsiders still believe that A.A. members need extraordinary moral strength and willpower to manage to go without alcohol. Those of you who are reading this book must believe me: the full A.A. experience is a dynamic, enthusiastic, lively, enriching adventure; we meet lots of friends, we celebrate anniversaries, we organize trips to our conventions, we receive many telephone calls and try to guide newcomers as best we can; in short, we are no longer alone; we move in a kind of whirlwind of love that would make anybody envious.

Finally, wanting to live in the present—twenty-four hours at a time—in no way implies that we are afraid to look back at the past or fear to project into the future. On the contrary, it shows that we have fully accepted our past as a life experience, tough at times, no doubt, but also fraught with meaningful lessons for us and for others; as a legacy of life, full of riches, as a story over which we no longer feel we have to shed tears. As far as the future is concerned, we don't have to worry about it since we have put it in God's hands, and we know it carries a promise of happiness and peace. We are convinced that living the day to the fullest is the best way to do God's will, as well as the best guarantee of sound moral health and of a peaceful future.

Tokens, Coins, Cakes

They say that the ancients marked the happy days of their lives with a white stone. It is the custom at A.A. to offer a token coin every three months for a year, and then to commemorate the first year of sobriety, and all those that follow, with an anniversary cake. We don't consider these as rewards—we are not children—but as acknowledgements, as forms of encouragement. I remember my first cake: my God, was I ever proud! To ignore success is to deprive people of the pat on the back they deserve. Of course, after many years, the sobriety anniversary cake will bring a more peaceful, quiet joy, but it is important to continue accepting the cake in front of all the members in order to bear witness. A.A. has been around for sixty years (1935-1995), and newcomers have to be given the opportunity to gauge the results. How could we possibly interest anyone in our programme if people are not convinced that, with A.A., they have a chance of remaining permanently sober? Those who have received a great deal must bear witness to it. That is hardly an option.

In Time, We Must Act... but Act We Must!

Some people always put things off. You must know some who never make a decision: it's too soon, it won't help to hurry, it can always wait! A spiritual life depends on a conscious decision: "Made a decision..." No one is going to do it for you. A.A. members procrastinate like everyone else. If someone asks them for advice on the steps, they will invariably answer: "Oh! not so fast, twenty-four hours at a time..." I am all for respecting the other's pace, but between that and always putting off until tomorrow, there's a difference. Bill W., who was well aware of the turtle syndrome, exclaimed one day: "Easy does it, but do it!" If you have not started your spiritual journey, go ahead, make a decision; ask questions, discuss it, seek... and you shall find. There is no other way. Besides, all the things we are hoping for—temperance, peace, to live and let live, to act simply, with judgment, patience and gentleness, etc.—are they not the fruit of a spiritual life? Deep down, you know it!

CONCLUSION

We have tried to show how, in the chaotic world of alcoholism, authentic spiritual values can reestablish a degree of order, peace, and harmony. Could we not deduce from this that the same principles could bring an answer to the anguish of the world, a consolation for all its miseries, and the love it so badly needs?

The world today is suffering from a dearth of spiritual values. These are necessary, not for the greater glory of God, but for everybody's greater good and happiness. It seems to me that if human beings saw in spiritual values their own happiness, they would find more of an incentive to live by them in this immediate result than in the ever so remote "greater glory of God". The greatest commandment, according to Jesus, is the love of God and neighbour. This commandment is not meant for God's happiness "first", but for ours. Men and women do not abide by this rule: they fight, they kill one another, exploit each other, take one another hostage; fathers and mothers weep over the assassination of their children... God sees our misery and pleads with us: "Love one another as I have loved you." Yet the world never ceases to cry out for love; think of all the songs about love and sharing, the T-shirts and caps with the inscription *Love*, the signs, graffiti and posters everywhere calling for love, peace, justice! Yet, how could men and women "as they are" find within themselves the strength to love? Study history; you will be edified. You learn love from love. Men and women will not know how to love until they turn to love. God Himself was not exempt from this rule; He had to learn love from Love: "As my Father has loved me, so also have I loved you." (Jn 5-9) Otherwise, we shall never love but those who love us, never greet anyone but our friends, never do good but in return for good done unto us; and we shall hate those who hate us, fight our enemies and return evil for evil. Should that disconcert us? Not in the least! It's only human! We might as well resign ourselves to the fact that, on his own, man's generosity will never go beyond the narrow confines of self-interest: me, my family, my relatives, my friends, my country, my race, my business, my success, my fortune! As for the rest of the world, let them paddle their own canoe! Without spiritual values, I see no real happiness for either individuals or society. And these spiritual values will have to emphasize a God of Love and the personal and collective happiness that would result from it. The world is so much in need of love! So much more in need of love than of sermons.

In the past, moral laws were laid down, orders issued and we obeyed. Today, the modern pragmatic approach requires that we first be informed of the practical consequences, in our personal lives, of the line of conduct about to be imposed upon us. Shouldn't morality be explained to a wider audience instead of just being imposed? Why not use mass media? Are the Churches making enough use of television? How is it that discussions pertaining to divorce, cohabitation before marriage, abortion, euthanasia, drugs, alcoholism, suicide, crime are the result of private initiatives by people who, no doubt, mean well, but who are more interested in establishing facts than in promoting spiritual values? Of course, mass is televised on Sundays... which does more for the glory of God than for the need for enlightenment and guidance in the simple man. Couldn't the Church, like Christ, leave the Temple and come down into the streets? Main street is no longer on the shores of Lake Tiberius: you get to it through your T.V. screen!

But perhaps the networks prefer to stay away from such issues. I don't know; I am merely asking the question. Many a worthwhile program has seen its air time reduced, or its budget slashed, or has simply been taken off the air.

Assuming that the difficulties arise from the television networks themselves, couldn't all the religious denominations get together, either to buy time or to set up their own studio from which to broadcast, even for just a few hours a day?

I dream of a Church that would get more involved in the world of those who do not read much, those who are told on millions of screens that happiness is "buying now and paying later." Who will take their side? What wretchedness!

We could well object that none are as deaf as those who don't want to hear, and that preaching on television amounts to preaching in the desert! Who knows? It's true that nothing is more disconcerting than the attitude of some middle-aged men and women towards religious values; one would think that, at their age, they would have gone beyond Armani suits, fashionable gossip and the inevitable displays on the cocktail circuit. But they haven't. They are basically decent people, but they continue to mask their misery, their loneliness and isolation; very religious people in their day, somehow, somewhere, they lost love. "Where did you lose this love? No one knows. There is only one area where you must look... and if love is lost, where did you see it last?" Search, deep down in your heart, for your early childhood. Don't you find there a breath of fresh air... a feeling of affection? Remember the crib: the Child, Mary and Joseph; and don't forget the ox... or the little donkey! Even today, when, on Christmas Eve, you hear "Come, all ye faithful...", what is that nostalgia that moves you in the very depths of your soul? What is it, when you walk with your arms full of gifts, that thrills you with anticipation and hastens your steps through the snow? What if on this same Christmas Eve, you had stayed at home alone: why should tears have welled up in your eyes as you admired the tree? It's because long ago there was love, and somehow, it was lost. You must find it, there, in the child's heart.

"Truly I say to you, whoever does not receive the Kingdom of God like a child shall not enter it." (Mk 10:15). Jesus is not saying that God will close the gates on those who have not accepted the Kingdom as children. He is saying that the great, the proud, the clever don't even knock at the gates; they don't even want to enter, only to be bored... not for the time being, anyway. No doubt, they will come later, when they will have suffered enough and depleted their resources in the process; when, bereft of everything, they will have become like little children, the "poor" of the Kingdom. I feel a twinge of pain when I think that some, among those I love, might never consent to knock at the gates of the Kingdom. This very thought might have prompted Jesus to go from door to door: "I stand at your door and knock..." in case you forgot! Compare God's humility with our self-importance! Jesus doesn't say: "Knock at my door, and I shall open..." but "I stand at your door and knock..."

Who knocks on doors? Those in need, those who ask a favour from you. Does it mean that "opening our heart to God" is doing Him a favour? Exactly! Because, you know, His Love is infinitely greater than ours.

In the Gospel, Jesus stresses the fact that God loves us like a Father, just like a father and a mother love their children. But we become sons and daughters of God only by accepting Jesus as our Brother. Through Christ, who is responsible for our participation in the New Covenant, we have been reconciled with the Father and brought into His love again; Jesus is our Redeemer. Our good deeds would not be enough. Neither the prodigal son, nor Mary Magdalene were accepted for their good works, as far as I know. If it were merely a question of justice, no one would be saved. Luckily for us, there is love.

This book presents but the first step of a spiritual journey: our turning to God and believing that He loves us, no matter who we are; becoming imbued with the idea that God's Love is gratuitous and we don't have to deserve it. God is, or He is not. If God is, then it is impossible for Him not to be. Now, God is Love, and hence He can never not love us. The only time Love fails to reach us is when we refuse to be loved. Accepting to be loved! That is the first step in a spiritual experience that is authentic, because it unfolds in the heart, where love is. This experience is often the privilege of desperate souls, of the lowly and the poor in spirit; they are all the more open to the experience of complete gratuitousness in love as they think they "deserve" nothing. "In this sense, it happens that sin and even vice are the most profound way of experiencing a significant encounter with God our Savior. Provided one accepts that salvation must come from Another." No love is authentic unless it is unmotivated. Those who believe that they deserve Love, that they are worthy of it, end up thinking that God owes them something. They don't know what love is; they are merely keeping accounts!

If this book has helped, in even the slightest measure, to imbue you with the gratuity of God's love for you, then I have not written in vain: my deepest wishes have been fulfilled and my heart is content.

As for the religious experience, Jesus will show you the way. All Mary Magdalene did at the outset was to take a few steps towards Him. Many of us have gone back to the Church and the Sacraments, sometimes helped by the experience of "intensive meetings", comparable to weekend retreats. Even among the most reticent participants at the beginning, many were profoundly touched. I cannot urge you too strongly to participate in these. Others like to join prayer groups like the Charismatics, Jacob's Well, etc. The Cursillo appeals to some. And also—when one becomes attached to Christ again—going back to Confession and to the ceremony of Bread and Wine provides the answer to a gentle call. (Certain Christian denominations do not celebrate these Sacraments.)

I cannot end this book without expressing my gratitude to the many brothers and sisters for all the help they gave me. A large number of A.A. meetings are held on premises that belong to religious communities. Their discretion is exemplary; never do they attempt in any way to impose their presence or their way of seeing things. And on a more personal level, they spend countless hours listening and giving advice. In my own case, I owe a great deal to the Jesuits, the Sisters of Providence, Sisters of Charity, Sisters of the Holy Cross. I also know of the hospitality offered by the Benedictines and the Trappists of Oka, to name a few. For their hospitality, their devotion and warm friendship, my most sincere thanks.

However, for reasons difficult to explain, many, though attached to Christ, ignore religious observances. Later on, they may come back to the practices of their childhood. It may take years, but it is a fond hope I express. Some, deeply wounded by life, will continue to shy away from religious practice and will be difficult to tame; and then there is the fringe group of those whose status within the Church keeps them, for a time, from strictly adhering to religious observance.

In the meantime, we can open our hearts to love. When I was young, I heard for the first time a song that I found so beautiful, so sweet that, whenever I hear it, I associate it with the idea of giving oneself up to Christ's love. I'm talking about *Sad Song*, music by Henri Duparc, lyrics by Jean Lahor. I cannot resist the urge to reproduce the entire text of the song which I like to call *Giving oneself to love* :

Deep down in your heart,
the moonlight is slumbering,
The soft light of a summer moon.
To escape from life and its distractions
I plunge into its quiet pool.

I shall forget the aches and pains
In your arms, my Love,
My sad heart and my thoughts
Are lulled, in the safety of your arms.

You will hold my aching head,
And sometimes, you will

Sing me a ballad,
A ballad about both of us.

And in your eyes filled with sadness,
I shall drink your love,
So much love and tenderness
That perhaps I shall be healed.

A splendid invitation to tenderness, calm, and peace: to love. God wants us to find calm, peace and inner harmony; to enter that place within us where He dwells; to heed the deepest, most pressing calls of our being, so that our desires, our dreams, all our aspirations will be fulfilled. All this doesn't happen automatically; we have far to go before we become detached from our pride and selfishness, from the faintest glimmer of resentment towards whatever or whomever, parents, educators, religious or political principles, questions of race or language, until nothing remains.We cannot hope to speak effectively about love as long as there persists in our hearts the slightest resentment, the least bitterness, the smallest tendency to criticize and condemn. We will also need much time to stop wanting "to prove something to ourselves", to stop wishing to absolutely "assert ourselves" on the outside. It is possible to give of ourselves to others out of love, and at the same time, out of a need to assert ourselves, and that's fine. But to reach the point where we can give solely out of love is even better.

The more we evolve, the more we become aware of our insignificance, of our emptiness. But isn't it because of this very emptiness that we shall be filled with God's Presence? The more we depend on God, the less we need to assert ourselves. We shall become "in"-dependent: only within ourselves can we find the confirmation of what we are. But we shall have to be very careful in our quest for a new life style not to wrong anyone. Not to "wrong" as opposed to "hurt": it is practically impossible to live without hurting someone around us: those who hang on to you, and who have decided that you will live for them alone; those who exploit you, who manipulate you, who suffocate you with their excessive love. To set oneself free from others does not take place overnight; it takes a long time, and much love. It must begin with setting oneself free from within, from one's own selfishness and dependence. Would you be able to live alone? I am not suggesting that you should—especially if you are married and have children—I am merely asking if you could? Would you be happy alone? Could you find within yourself alone your source of happiness? To be free of others does not necessarily mean to leave them—it could become necessary—but it means not to "absolutely" need them. We should never relate to others because we need them, but because we love them—that isn't the same thing. Don't be afraid; this doesn't mean you are doomed to living alone: there are so many people to love! It means that we should detach ourselves from others, so that we may love them better, gratuitously. To love this way is to become more and more attached to God who is present within us; it means finding—in a certain zone of our inner self, where we must search—the Answer to our need for love, the Source of all Love: the Great Love! This is where we make permanent contact, and all our life becomes a prayer; this is when we shall know how to love, not through need, but for love's sake! Then our loves will be lasting.

God be with you!

WORKS CITED

Alcoholics Anonymous, Alcoholics Anonymous World Services, New York, 1955.

Dowling, R.P.E., S.J., *Alcoholics Anonymous,* a lecture.

Dyer, Wayne W., *Your Erroneous Zones*, Funk and Wagnalls, New York, 1976.

Ensemble, (religious education cards), n° 4, Amiens,1967.

Hétu, Jean-Luc, *Quelle foi?*, Leméac, Montréal, 1978.

Hypoglycaemia and Me, Adrenal Metabolic Research Society of the Hypoglycaemia Foundation, 153 Pawling Avenue, Troy, N. Y. 12180, Marylin H. Light, 1973.

Kessel, Joseph, *Avec les Alcooliques Anonymes*, Gallimard, "L'Air du temps", Paris.

Low Blood Sugar, Karpart Publishing, P.O. Box 5348, Cleveland, Ohio, 44101.

La Psychologie moderne de A à Z. Comprendre-savoir-agir, Centre d'étude et de la promotion de la lecture, Paris, 1967.

Rogers, Carl, *Le Développement de la personne*, Dunod, Paris, 1968.

The A.A. Way of Life, Alcoholics Anonymous World Services, New York, 1972.

The Shoes of the Fisherman, film, Prod. George Englund.

Achevé d'imprimer
en mars 1996
sur les presses de
Métrolitho

Imprimé au Canada — Printed in Canada